STRAIGHT FROM THE HORSE'S MOUTH

~

by

Roly Armitage, DVM, VS

Title: **Straight From the Horse's Mouth**

by: ROLY ARMITAGE, DVM, VS

ISBN-13: 978-1726311465

ISBN-10: 1726311465

Published by Roly Armitage

Cover, layout and editing by Mary Montague, m3m@rogers.com

Dedication

I would like to dedicate this book entitled *Straight From the Horses Mouth* to my good friend Bill Galvin.

Bill, a member of The Horse Racing Hall of Fame, has without doubt, done more than anyone regarding the promotion of the sport, in both the Thoroughbred and Standardbred categories.

He is an outstanding author, writer, and historian of horse racing in Canada and throughout the world.

During the writing of this book I have called on him many times to get pertinent information and facts regarding people and horses. I have thanked him many times and herewith, I thank you Bill, one more time.

I would further like to recognize the tremendous efforts made by my editor Mary Montague, for, at times, putting up with the *sometimes* cranky author of this book. He was in the habit of emailing her paragraphs and stories in a non-chronologicial order at daily and weekly intervals. She was still miraculously able to decipher the material and come up with an outstanding presentation of this horse-oriented subject.

Raley

Message from the Author

This is my third book. As most of you may already know my first book *The Way it Was and Now* dealt with my life and experiences from childhood to the present time. The second, *Now, About Yesterday* was a collection of vignettes  about places I have been and people I have known. I have been very fortunate that during my lifetime I have met many very interesting people and even more fortunate in that a great number of them have become my friends. I have been truly blessed.

I wish to thank those of you who purchased the first two books and I have appreciated the positive feedback that I received from them.

It is hoped that that you will enjoy this book, *Straight From the Horse's Mouth,* my third and probably my last, venture into the literary world.

Contents

Introduction

Unfortunately, other than to mention them, we are unable to cover every presentation of the Horse Kingdom herein. Such diverse interests as Horse Pulling Contests, Thoroughbred Racing, Standardbred Racing, Quarter Horse Racing, the Sport of Polo, Horse Jumping Contests, Western Saddle Riding, English Saddle Mounts, Dressage Presentations, Ceremonial Presentations, police horses, the RCMP Ride, Hackney ponies and horses, and various Children's Ponies, are all here for man's working assistance, riding, pleasure, and otherwise. My purpose in this book is just to pay tribute to and enjoy their existence, grace and beauty.

• • •

The horse and prehistoric man - now in this year of 2018 I realize I should be using the term woman as well as man, although it is proven that the pre-historic term *man* was plural and meant humans and so in the interests of expediency and with apologies to the fairer sex I am using the term *man* in the following discussion.

One has to think that the horse, because of its excessive strength was adopted by man for their use in the development of civilization as we know it. I include donkeys and mules in the same category as the horse because they are of the same species and possess strength in varying degrees but still less than the horse.

Most people wonder how the pyramids were built when we all know that no modern backhoes or huge cranes were in existence at that time, and, even if they were, they could not have been run without today's methods for adapting fuel for energy, none of which was available then.

One thing we do know is that there were horses, simple pulley systems and man - all available. This could very likely have been the only source of energy in the construction of the pyramids and the other fabulous prehistoric structures that still stand at this time. The foregoing concerning the structure of the pyramids is my assumption and not the scientific answer - nor is there anyone alive who was there at the time to tell us how it was actually done. *Give me your version if you think a horse was not involved and I am willing to listen.* However, one thing we do know for certain was that the donkey was in existence 2000 years ago when Jesus walked this earth as he is recorded as having ridden one. So, I believe we are safe in assuming that the donkey and the horse, his much stronger relative from the same species, was not only in existence but actively involved in pyramid construction during Egypt's Old Kingdom era 4500 years ago.

Roly Armitage

Background

When the first settlers came to the new world they were entering a land where the aboriginals had, since the beginning of time, been functioning as a hunting and gathering society. The settlers' main asset was the knowledge that had been acquired during society's evolution in the countries from which they came. Using that knowledge, these pioneers set about clearing land and building homes. They acquired horses from the aboriginals or by capturing and taming ones that were running wild to help in those tasks. The horse, without any doubt, proved to be a very loyal and indispensable worker. More than that, and possibly because of that, the human admiration and love of this animal has been contagious. As a veterinarian, I have observed and been involved in the welfare of the horse and its proximity and association with humans. It is my desire to expose and portray these observations, characteristics and the comradery that exists between both species.

From the very first basic horse, man, through breeding and desire has developed the horse into variable sizes and confirmations to suit their specific needs. Be it the clean-legged black or grey Percherons, the bay and white Clydesdales with hairy white ankles, mane and tail, to the beige coloured Belgians, all developed for their massive size and weight to do hard work, or the more scaled-down models of size and confirmation for riding, racing, or domestic uses, humans have been involved in their evolution.

There is also a horse that was developed by controlled cross-breeding of selected individuals and that is a black coloured horse called 'Canadian.' This horse is used as a so-called dual-purpose horse as its size is good for riding or pulling a buggy like the Mennonite people, for instance, use to go from point to point. It is also very muscular and can be hitched with a team of large horses draw a heavy load. They are a relatively friendly breed and cooperate with man's direction when needed.

• • •

Horse Racing Vocabulary

Before we get into any in-depth discussion about the horse I would like to touch upon some of the words and phrases that are familiar to *horse* people but may seem strange to others. Not all are found in Websters Dictionary. It's called 'Horse Talk.'

The Racetrack

The average and customary distance that is used in Canadian racing is one mile. The size of a racetrack is described as being a half mile, or 5/8ths or 7/8ths, which means the distance around the track one time. In case of a *half-mile track* such as the one at Flamboro, Ontario, and the race would commence in front of the grandstand and go around twice and finish in front of the grandstand. Racing on a *5/8ths mile track*, such as the one at Rideau Carleton in Ottawa, the start would be on the backstretch at a point 3/8ths of a mile around to the finish post in front of the grandstand and then one more complete trip around the track for a distance being 5/8ths of a mile. Hence 3/8ths and 5/8ths make up the mile. In the case of a 7/8ths mile track such as Mohawk at Campbellville Ontario, the race would commence 1/8th of a mile *before the finish line* in front of the grandstand and then one full turn of the track for a distance of 7/8ths, therefore 1/8th plus the 7/8th makes up one full mile.

Timing

During a race the announcer who is the person who verbally calls each race talks about the times in minutes and seconds. You get his first call at the quarter-mile post in seconds and next on the time at the half-mile post, then at the three quarter mile post and finally at the finish, when he will yell "TIME OF THE MILE one fifty eight and three." The meaning of this in horse language is *'One minute, and fifty eight point three fifths of a second.'* This time would be abbreviated as 1.58.3 on paper.

Positions on the Track

When horse people are talking to one another they will use terms such as at the half or at the quarter when discussing position during a race. Some horses are tremendous *leavers* from the start where others are slow at the start but are good at so called *coming from the back of the pack* at the finish while some of the fast leavers will tire at the end. You will note that Standardbreds in sulky racing always find a position on the rail as soon as possible at the start of a race and usually don't move out and around those in front of them until about the half mile pole because it is much further getting home from a *parked out position* meaning on the outside where the distance home is 56 feet further than staying on the rail.

Hub Rail

Speaking about the term **hub rail**: there used to be a wooden rail the same height as the hub of the sulky wheel around the sides of the racetrack but several drivers and horses have been killed or seriously injured by being crowded and forced over the top during an accident. May I state emphatically that I take the credit for having the rail removed and replaced with a white plastic moveable picket every twelve feet being used as a guide and there has not been a death that I am aware of in the past 30 years as a result thereof.

Positions on Track

There are many terms used that relate to racing and may not be understood by non-participants. Things like drafting and sitting in the two hole which is also said to be the best position to be in as the horse in front is cutting the mile and the wind while the horse immediately behind the leader has less resistance and psychologically it gives this horse an immediate impetus when you pull it out to pass the horse in front when in the home stretch. Horses trailing to the half mile post have a big advantage if the front end goes extra fast and they tend to tire at the end while those behind are fresh and having not been used too much at this point can kick into gear and drive on and become a winner.

Position in the race – last line

Each part of a second is described as a fifth of a second, or divided into five parts. In a race that goes in two minutes, the horse is considered to have covered five body lengths in one second, or one length in one fifth of a second.

Gait

All horses have a gait such as pacers whose two legs on one side move forward at the same time, while a trotter is diagonally gaited meaning the left front and right hind legs move forward at the same time. If a horse, at any time breaks stride from a trotting gait or a pacing gait, and goes on a run called a gallop, such as how a thoroughbred horse races, then the horse is disqualified..

When horses are galloping they are in a natural runaway gait where they are in the air most of the time. This is a single footed gait where every time they are in the air, they then land on the fore foot which is the lead leg in front and it lands there first followed by two, three, four in that order so every time they are in the air they land one front foot at a time, such as the one, two, three four rhythm. It is also described as a *lopping gait*, such as one, two, three, four, leaping, landing, and repeat. This is a very fast gait.

Again in the standardbred gait the pacer has two feet on the ground at all times and switches to the two feet on the opposite time in forward motion while a trotter also has two feet going foreword at the same time but the two feet are diagonal, right front, left hind.

When a standardbred breaks gait it can be put back on stride and not be disqualified as long as it is taken back by the driver and did not gain ground while on the run, or so called gallop.

Up on the Bit

We speak of horses being up on the bit, which means the driver has a good firm hold of the horse which makes it very easy to steer as all controls of the animal is done in this manner.

Spitting the Bit

We use the term 'spits the bit' when a horse gives up in a race.

• • •

Horses are all called foals at birth, the standardbred female is called a **filly** for the first three years in its life and then called a **mare** after its third year. The standardbred male is a **colt** for the first two years of life and a **horse** or **stallion** after its third year. In the case of thoroughbreds a female is called a filly until its fourth year and the male is called a colt until its third year and then a horse or stallion in its fourth year. When and if a stallion is castrated (testicles surgically removed) the animal then is called a **gelding**. In some cases in male foals the testicles may not have yet descended into the scrotum, or only one may have descended. This is termed to be a *cryptorchid*. They sometimes descend on their own and other times veterinary intervention may be needed. A foal with this condition is not to be confused with a gelding. A male horse with just one testicle descended is called a ridgling.

Deviating from the racing aspect itself, after the owner of a mare has studied her breeding and confirmation aspects, which stallion she should be bred to must be decided. Then a lot of decisions have to be made. First, and foremost, is your mare qualified within the industry to have the qualities and breeding to convey to its offspring so that they will have the ability to compete under very competitive circumstances? If it does, to whom regarding which available stallion do you disclose your decision? Once, after much careful deliberation, that decision has been made, you make application to the breeding farm or owner of the stallion. If you are accepted, you arrange for the breeding to take place at a given time.

You or your veterinarian decides on the ovulation date and phones for the semen. It comes by AIR Canada or other air carrier, and you promptly pick it up, take it home and have the mare infused with the semen. *Alas*, after a few days the veterinarian, with a long, well-lubricated plastic glove on, does a manual examination via the rectal area and states that the mare is in foal and a *future champion* has begun the journey to its birth.

Normally under all horse racing conditions male horses race only with their own sex, be they stallions or castrated stallions called *geldings*, and alternately fillies and mares race separately with their own kind. As for speed, stallions have a small advantage over geldings because of the fact that the hormone testosterone does help in giving them strength. However, when training as young stallions, often in company with fillies they spend too much of their time looking sideways at the young fillies and less time learning to become good race horses. Thus, because most stallions have this tendency to be very fractious and consequently are harder to train, it is customary to castrate them unless their breeding is of such a high calibre that eventually they could be good breeding prospects.

The birth of a foal is a very heart warming experience. For the owner of the foal, this event it is brought about by natural copulation or, more commonly now as alluded to above, by controlled artificial means where the semen is collected and infused into the female at the correct time when ovulation is natural *or* brought about by controlled medical intervention. Medical intervention is to ensure that birth will happen in the month of February so that the foal will have almost a year to grow and develop before it will be designated as a one-year-old because, regardless of when the foal is born, it becomes a so-called yearling on the 1st of January following its birth and a two-year-old on the next new year's day. The gestation period is approximately eleven months.

In nature this ovulation is controlled by the length of the daylight hours, hence during the longest day in mid-June the mare would then attract the stallion - oh, he wouldn't dare miss the event *because he would be cruising as he knows that this is the time for him to do his duty and, as with humans, the total act can be quite pleasurable.* Thus, the miracle of gestation begins with birth happening eleven months later. The foal would be born on a bright, warm sunny day in May when the mare would be outside in nature with green grass and pleasant surroundings.

Now however, considering the excessive costs involved in horse ownership, births are invariably in a controlled, clean and in as sterile as possible box stall with the owner or veterinarian in close proximity to ensure safe delivery. Iodine is usually applied to the navel area to prevent infection. It then is best to stand away and let the mare and foal learn to associate with one another. The foal should get the first milk *(colostrum)* as soon as possible as this milk is laxative in nature and contains antibodies, minerals and vitamins and proteins all in very digestible forms to ensure the foal gets a good start in life.

All horses at birth are really wild animals and are naturally lovers of freedom until they gain respect for humans. They invariably strongly resist handling and, since they are creatures of habit, other than early handling and care, the foal runs freely with its mother, hopefully on grass. The foal is weaned from its mother anytime after the 4th or 5th month of life and then it is raised separately or together with other weaned foals.

When the foal becomes a late yearling, at about 18 months of age, it is then separated and specialized training begins to prepare it for its specific duties in life. There are several avenues. Horses used in saddlery are trained in the English or Western style. In racing there are three categories, Quarter Horse, and Thoroughbred, both trained with riders on their backs and at a galloping or extended gait, and Standardbreds, which are hitched to a cart or so-called sulky upon which the driver sits in control. There are two Standardbred gaits (methods of moving style) *Trotters*, who have a diagonal gait such as the left front and right hind move forward together, and then the right front and left hind follow. The other gait is *Pacing* or amble, where both feet on the same side move forward at the same time. All race horse training takes about eight or nine months to complete the series of training prior to race time. Before they can race they have to be subjected to qualifying speed times being observed by Stewards or Judges who do the timing.

In the work horse class of horses they are usually in pairs with a long wooden shaft or so called tongue which runs from the vehicle, up between the two individuals to a neck yoke that is attached to the collars that are around the horses' necks and part of their harness. Horses, like humans, are subjected to various vaccinations and deworming and are fed a properly balanced and energizing feed.

The horse while outside on grass will eat for 14 hours whereas under feed control a 1000 pound horse eats approximately 20 pounds of choice hay a day and about one to one and a half pounds of 14% protein grain a day per 100 pounds of horse. The grain portion should vary with amount of work and the flesh condition of the horse's rib area. In most cases horses are kept in stalls with clean bedding, using either straw or wood shavings and receive excellent care and handling by qualified grooms. They sleep at varying times lying down but their suspensory ligaments are so constructed that they can sleep while in standing position.

Speaking of the Standardbred horse - when the foal is up and about, the birth is announced by the owner, by informing Standardbred Canada, the governing body. An agent comes to the farm and draws a blood sample and, using liquid nitrogen, a series of numbers is branded under the mane on the right side. This painlessly kills the pigment and legible letters show up in white in a few months. The blood sample is DNA'd and, since the father and mother have already been DNA'd, absolute proof is now established that this animal does have the blood lines of its very important parents. Also after a race the winning horse and one other at random are blood and urine tested for possible drugging. On a given night the presiding judge often calls for the veterinarian in the paddock to blood test every horse in *a selected at random* race. Furthermore, every driver on every racing program is subjected to a sobriety test before the races proceed. Thus, every patron can be assured that the horse in every race is that horse, because each and every horse in every race has been authenticated by the paddock judge after having read the identifying markings under the mane. All of these conditions apply to all horse racing in Canada; the thoroughbreds are identified by a legible ink tattoo under the upper lip.

In Ontario and several other provinces in Canada we have two and three-year-old races known as *Sires Stakes*. In this case all stallions in Ontario are listed as being eligible to sire foals born from mares also standing in Ontario. When the foal is in its yearling year the owner makes a deposit of about $700 before a specific date and this makes the colt or filly eligible to race in the Ontario Sires Stakes program. Then by about March another sustaining payment is made as two year olds for those horses who are intended to race in the program that year. Likewise, this occurs as three-year-olds. When payments are made, the owner declares the sex and racing conditions such as Pace or Trot and payments are put into the specific race pot. If your horse does not race then the money deposited is, of course, left in the pot for those that do race. Further, there is a starting payment that also is part of the purse. There are two divisions within the stakes program. There is a Gold series that owners enter and these horses will race against the best. If the owner thinks his candidate is not up to that calibre then there is the Grass Roots series which goes for less money and the entry fee is less. After they race in this lesser series and they do well they can move up to Gold in ensuing races, and vice versa for those who felt that Gold was out of their class can go to Grass Roots.

Speaking of the purses for the sires stakes – for the Gold Series there would be $225,000 allocated for purses in each of 5 races at a specific track. Races are allocated at possibly Grand River Raceway one night, then Mohawk Raceway the next, then at

Georgia Downs at Barrie the next then possibly back to Mohawk. Usually there would be three divisions of the purse for the first race as there would be three races of 10 entries, so the money would be divided and we would go for $75,000 per division and the winner would get half of the purse, as the money is divided this way, 50 % to the winner, 25% to the second horse, and then 12%, 8%, and finally 5% for the 5th horse and, alas, all those 6th, 7th, 8th, 9th, and 10th get the saying, 'Enjoy your journey.'

If there are only two races of 10 horses then the purse would be split in two and you would race for $100,000 plus per race so winning can be lucrative. At the end of the five races a grand final would go to the top ten horses who got the most points in the Gold or Grass Roots Series. In the case of the Gold it would be a purse of approximately $250,000 and decidedly less for the Grassroots. Please understand that these figures are approximate but close. Following these Stakes series and as the winners become four-year-olds they would either have a lot of buyers for them or alternately the fillies, now mares, would be bred to an Ontario sire with intent of getting a good price for their yearling at future scheduled horse sales.

Aside from these Sire Stake races the industry has many more stake races such as Breeders Crown, Canadian Pacing Derby open to the world, The Trotting Classic, and many more major races.

Thoroughbred Racing has all and more than the Standardbred industry including not only the several Staking series but the world famous Queen's Plate and other renowned Classics.

The whole racing industry is a heavy employment environment. Think of the veterinarians, drivers, jockeys, large seed and feed sales of grain and hay, trucks and trailers, fuel sales, construction and maintenance of racing tracks, administration people, food outlets, farm training tracks and their established maintenance, and it goes on and on. Some years ago the Government of Ontario decided to go into the lottery casino business and to prevent spending big dollars on facilities they approached the race tracks to be the source of the Casinos base and from the gross profits they gave a share of the gross profits to the host track, the local municipality and 20% to the horse people for purses. There was a contract signed by the province and everything sailed along just great and the province alone took in more than a billion dollars a year. Race tracks flourished, horse people invested deeply into new horses and breeding establishments brought new stallions and municipalities enjoyed this new money.

Then after 12 years into the contract Premier McGuinty decided he wanted all the profit and informed everyone that the gig was up and gave one year's notice of cessation of the contract. Obviously everybody was financially hurt and many horses were sold or in some cases sent for slaughter and breeding establishments had to transfer horses, mostly to other jurisdictions which saw a tremendous loss. The outcome was that several grooms and others who knew no other method of employment no longer had a place to live, as they had in many cases, lived at the track beside their cares.

Time however marched on and after this disaster the government saw its mistake and then tried to in some way or otherwise compensate everyone for their losses by putting a sum of money to be distributed. Breeders suffered tremendously and at this present time are in court, charging the government for breach of contract. A new amalgamated racing management has been established in Ontario and things seem to be coming to a more stable position although a number of grassroots small-farm training tracks throughout rural Ontario have disappeared.

• • •

As discussed in detail earlier, the horse has proven its value on many different fronts. Locally in Ottawa, where I live, it contributed during the early years to clearing the land for our forefathers, and it was essential in the building of the Rideau Canal, which was completed in 1832, and was intended to provide a secure supply route from Montréal to

Kingston, thus avoiding the vulnerable St. Lawrence River route in case there would be further American aggression. The War of 1812 when the Canadians beat back the invading Americans was still fresh in everyone's mind.

The canal is considered one of the greatest engineering feats of the 19th century. It was a massive undertaking under the capable direction of Colonel John By and is 125 miles long. Rivers, lakes and ponds had to be connected to complete the project. Actually 12 miles of land had to be landscaped to complete the waterway from Kingston to Ottawa, and the *so-called* draft or heavy horse did the majority of the work along with the thousands of men involved. Now, of course, it is declared an historical accomplishment. I, only bring this project to the fore to again illustrate the horse's historical significance and the understanding that none of this could have been accomplished without it. Likewise, in the past, man's only conveyance from *A* to *B* in summer and severe winter conditions prior to mechanical means was accomplished only with the horse.

• • •

Today with the racing industry being where it is in our society, with all the enjoyment and its established position in our way of life, there are people – so-called activists – who are forever declaring the racing of horses to be cruel and should be abolished. If they only knew what trainers and owners of these horses know – that the desire to win in a given race by a given horse is so obvious that when someone might ask a driver regarding his abilities in bringing about the win, the driver's response would most likely be, "A child could have driven this horse." In other words the horse enjoys the opportunity to beat its competition. We all know and have observed a rather quiet horse under stable and daily jogging conditions, when seeing a change in daily routine by the appearance of a trailer, things that are done to get ready for an impending race, become anxious, excited and figity. It knows that it is race time and is just as knowledgeable as you are that things are about to happen and it doesn't speak, but what it's saying is, "Lets go! I'm ready!"

• • •

The water in the Rideau Canal hardly had time to flow and freeze between Kingston and Ottawa in 1832 when the general public, all owners of horses, established racing on the ice surface and this went on for years before the mechanization of travel. In 1979, Bill Galvin, then publicist and promotional person with the Canadian Trotting Association, the governing body of Standardbred Horses decided to bring racing back to the canal and contacted the City of Ottawa and the National Capital Commission.

Appearance

Horses come in many different colours and sizes. Regarding colours, the most prominent is a so-called *bay.* This can be can be a light or dark-brown shade. Another prominent colour is *black.* A *brown* horse is actually a black horse but the muzzle (front of the face) is brownish. We all know what a *grey* horse looks like but they are less common. Then we have *chestnut,* which is a usually a bright, shiny maroon colour. Then the *piebald,* which is of various colours, like white with red, black or brown patches – known also as *pintos* or *paints.* These are associated more with quarter horses. All these various colours make them sort of stand out in appearance.

When all is said and done the average Standardbred or Thoroughbred is *bay* in colour. Now we also have *white* spots in various places like the feet and ankles or legs. The face has so-called stars of white between the eyes but often this white can be seen as a *blaze* down the face or just a white nostril. Manes and tails are generally very black and flowing but at times the ends can lighten up a bit. All horses have long black hairs under their jaws and these should never be trimmed as they have a feeling effect for letting them know where their face is when eating or drinking.

Size

The size of horses is another subject but fundamentally we have bred them to be different sizes and shapes depending on the type of work or performance we expect from them. The height of horses is described by using the word '*Hands.*' A hand is considered to be 4 inches and the horse is measured from the ground up going vertically from just behind the front legs to the spot directly where the mane starts on the horse's back and is called '*The Pole.*' The average height of a horse is 14.2 to 17.2 hands. A hand measurement term of 15 hands means 15 X 4 = 60 inches. Likewise the term 15.2 hands is 15 X 4 inches, plus 2 more inches, or a total of 62 inches high. Think about where the pole is on the horse and try to visualize it - think of seeing a horse with a western saddle with a large horn as part of its very front, then the Pole is directly in front of that - where the *Lone Ranger* would rest his hands when stopped and leaning forward.

Identification of and the Necessity For It

Prior to the methods we have now of having positive identification of a racing horse in a given condition and the reasons for making every effort in bringing this about, I will give you one example of why this condition was necessarily established. It was about 1975 when I was the Track Veterinarian at Connaught Park in Aylmer, Quebec and a stake race was being conducted on this given day. This race was for two-year-old colts and geldings who where born and trained in Quebec. It was one of a series of races for this particular group of horses and several legs of the event had already been held at various other tracks in the Quebec province.

There was one colt in the group who was having tremendous success and had won every leg of the series up to including this date at the Gatineau track. When a horse wins a given race in this series, it is subjected to a saliva test for drugging, and hence the subject came to the test area in the paddock and I proceeded to take the test. In conducting this test we used a long set of sterilized forceps and an equivalent sterile cloth swap material with which we collected a saliva sample which was then processed for shipping to a laboratory for testing. While carrying out this process I was alarmed to observe that this horse was a three year old according to his dental arrangement; I immediately called the presiding judges that this horse was three years old and was fraudulently unqualified to be in this series. The judge immediately called for a second opinion, which was carried out by another qualified veterinarian.

As a result, the owner was found guilty of fraudulently racing his horse, had to refund all winning monies from previous victories, paid a heavy monitory fine plus he was barred from owning or racing horses for life. His winning monies from previous victories was redistributed among the horses involved in previous stake races.

Now of course a lay person might ask the question, "How could you tell the age of the horse by his dental arrangement?" May I explain. When a foal is born the teeth are rudimentary and develop as it ages by having 10 incisor teeth dorsal and ventral (upper and lower). These teeth are snow white and the two inner teeth on the top row are pushed out and off by two natural and permanent teeth when the animal becomes two years old, likewise the next two teeth on either side of the middle two are pushed out and replaced by the next two permanent teeth when the colt or filly becomes three years old. This goes on yearly until all ten teeth, both upper and lower are replaced permanently. We then say that the subject then has a full and mature mouth at 5 years of age. We also can tell the age further by the fact that on the surface of the outside top incisor tooth, a brown line extends down starting at six years of age, is half way down at ten years and all the way down at twenty years old. Not every horse has this characteristic but most do in some order or fashion. It is only a guide, but a useful one.

During the testing of the above horse in question, the colt had the three-year-old version of dental presentation. There is then what we call a dental space between the incisors and the molar teeth of the colt or filly of about 4 inches, with the exception that the majority of horses has what we call we call *wolf teeth* – these are rudimentary single teeth located just in front of the first top molar tooth on both sides and are called rudimentary because in prehistoric times, back in nature, the horse had a sort of *fang* or very sharp tooth that extended out in a hooked, upward fashion, of each corner of their mouth for defensive purposes. Due to the horse then being domesticated, the use of the this tooth is long gone. However, since this rudimentary portion still exists and is in front of the first molar, where the driving *bit* of a race horse sits, then it has to be extracted to prevent the horse exhibiting distress and maybe carrying the head to one side or other in training. A horse's teeth continue to grow because in nature they are continually eating grass and grit and sand that eventually gets into the mouth which naturally grinds the teeth and keeps them the right length. Now because they are kept under controlled environmental conditions and eat softer foods it is mandatory that we keep an eye on the teeth by filing off the sharp edges when necessary.

Horses do not chew fibres as we humans do but they chew in a sideways motion which results in the lower molars on both sides becoming sharp on the inside while getting sharp on the outside of the top molars, and if left unattended can result in tongue lacerations.

Categories in racing

There are several very important categories involved in racing. First of all you need breeders who produce the horses, followed by owners who purchase them either privately or at established sales where the prices are determined by the bids from prospective owners. These prices are obviously determined by the extended pedigree of the horse – their ancestors and particularly of the sire (the father) and the dam (the mother) and what either of them have shown as individuals re: speed and age of when that was established but also the performance of their siblings. It is an in-depth study.

Confirmation is a very important factor when purchasing a horse. All their legs should be in the right place and lot of features such as a bright eye, width of the jaw for easy breathing, open nostrils, body shape and length, foot size and proper angles everywhere are all important factors to be considered in determining future ability. Today, due to the breeding, confirmation, and speed of their ancestors, the foals or offspring actually pace or trot during their early gaits because of natural inherited ability. Prior to that trainers had to add weights in different areas to the shoeing to accomplish a given gait.

The Foot

The foot of the horse is a very important part of the horse. There is a saying it the horse world, quote, *"No foot, No horse."* The care of horses' feet is left to the professional *farriers* who through extensive training and experience know what type of shoe each individual horse should wear under different circumstances. There are several conditions regarding foot or track conditions that determine the shoe the horse wears. For instance on icy conditions they weld sharp points on the shoe surface to avoid slipping, or more weight on the toe of the shoe to make the horse reach out, more or weight on the heel of the shoe to increase lift. The average weight of a shoe would be approximately two pounds and are in various shapes and surfaces depending on track conditions.

Shoeing

The normal movements of the horse's front feet are very important in propelling the horse forward. To correct any deviations from this normal forward motion, experienced farriers often do what we call corrective shoeing.

First of all, it is important to know that in nature there is an established normal movement of the foot. When the foot touches the ground, it lands on the heel sliding forward a few inches, then rolls forward having the foot landing flat on its surface. Then it rolls forward in an arc over the toe; the heel rises appropriately and the final thrust forward comes off the toe.

Normal shoeing of the foot is be as close to the normal surface of the foot as possible as its sole purpose is to prevent wear and damage to the sole of the foot while the horse is propelled at tremendous speeds during racing. If, however, the foot does not go forward in a normal fashion due to conformation and so on, it may go towards touching the opposite knee. Then, rather than having just a flat bottomed shoe which would not prevent the foot coming forward and sliding on an inward motion and touching the opposite knee, then we would use a shoe which had a raised ridge on the outside that would hold and delay the foot from not going in a straight line. Just common sense is applied. If for instance you wanted to have the horse raise the foot higher to go over the opposite knee then by adding a little weight to the heel of the shoe does help quite a bit.

It is not my intent to talk about the whole subject of corrective shoeing, because first of all it is not my area of expertise, but a farrier who is an expert and a specialist in this field can achieve wondrous results. One thing I do know is that turning the shoe backwards to add weight to a heel and having the toe open to break over faster is disastrous from a veterinary stand point because when the foot hits the ground the heel of the shoe cannot slide forward as it should due to the steel heel barrier. Thus the shock is transferred to the leg causing extreme pressure on leg tendons and the shoulder. I personally have frequently been called to a lame horse and found this type of shoeing to be absolutely a *no no*. In the horse racing world we often humorously state that if we can correct the front end of the horse then the backend will behave its self and come along okay.

The Grooms

When speaking of grooms one has to really categorize them, and for which I will explain later. Every girl or boy, be they part of an established racing family, stable, or not, must start at the bottom. These horses are all being kept under very artificial conditions from the horses natural state, and therefore they must be cared for, hand and foot. The horse is known to be a creature of habit and since we have taken the wild from them so to speak, the horse will henceforth learn its purpose in life as it is associated with people and everything that we teach them to do, and the horse adopts that as the norm. Start with the size of its stall, the best is 10 feet by 12 feet but lesser can be acceptable. The most important factor is that the stall be injury free where the walls have no 'nails' on the surface or any other thing on which it might injure itself. The horse should have a door where it can look out of to see and be seen. They love observing the actions of the stable hands and what is going on. It needs to be high enough that it can't get caught in if it raises up to frolic. Feeding and watering facilities should be away from this observing area.

Now that we have a good living quarters, the floor should be of an impervious nature to absorb urine, such as stone dust or sand to lessen undue wear or damage on its hooves and *not* concrete.

Now is where the **groom** comes into the picture. The bedding will be either wood shavings or natural wheat or oat straw. There is a proper way to do the daily cleaning of the stall. First remove the horse to another safe area. Now, with a pitch fork the clean material is thrown to the edge of the stall, and with a wheel barrow the wet bedding and feces are loaded into the cart and the central area brushed. Normally white lime is used to cover the wet contaminated area and then the original good bedding that was saved originally is thrown back, plus more new bedding is added to make things comfortable until the next day. Then the cartload of waste is removed to be dumped wherever the established point is and the horse is returned to its stall.

Those grooms who have learned the primary care of the domesticated horse are then ready to move on to more advanced areas. Here is where the separation takes place and we speak of grooms who are ordinary people with a basic training in life and have drifted to the environment of the racetrack and those who are truly dedicated. These individuals become so dedicated to their responsibilities that the care of their horses come hours before they care for themselves. They forget about the outside world and associate with their horse to the point they sleep in the same stall or the one adjacent thereto. Perhaps because of their isolated life style many of these individuals are oblivious to the outside world but no one can fault them regarding their efficient care of your horse or horses. They actually marry themselves to the job at hand.

This environment all came tumbling down when McGuinty pulled the plug on the casinos at tracks and the industry fell apart. As I stated previously owners got out of the business and the poor grooms became unemployed and many became wards of the state.

The Trainers

The trainers are the primary school teachers. First, where did they come from? They are young people, often the ones who sneaked up to the racetracks, unknown to their parents and peeked through the fences at the *goings-on* at tracks. This all fascinated them with the mysteries involved therein. They finally found their ways into the track and observed and made contacts. Horsemanship is a fascinating bond between man and horse. As these young people got older on their holidays they got jobs as grooms which entails the feeding and care of the horse. They got to learn the comradery that exists between the man and beast. It is actually like a disease and after you have been there and left, there is always a yearning to go back.

Apprentice trainers are usually grooms who have been outstanding in their duties and in the care of their responsibilities. The head trainers give them the opportunity to jog or exercise the horses they are in charge of. While this is going on they are being observed as to their ability in communicating with and their feeling for the animal in their care. These amateurs observe and learn from experienced trainers around them and eventually become *second trainers* for a year or two before becoming fully accomplished. Most future drivers came from the trainer ranks. Their abilities come from years and hundred of miles of sitting in a jog cart behind their trainees, observing the horses and correcting the faults or flaws as they are observed.

All these miles are trotted or paced to establish a flawless muscular gait before speed is asked for and you go from there asking for a little more speed each month over a nine-month period. You finally take your product to the racetracks to be judged for their ability in time trials.

The Driver and the Driver's Dress

From a safety and dress-oriented aspect, changes have been made regarding the former and present appearances of standardbred horse drivers at all North American and world-wide race tracks.

Modern-day outfit on left – original on right.

Originally drivers wore only colourful jackets with matching soft material peak caps and any kind of trousers. Today our drivers wear personally designed coloured jackets with white trousers along with an injury proof form-fitting flack vest thereunder. The original soft cap has now been replaced with a hard form-fitting helmet with an under-jaw strap and it is a mandatorily ordered condition to have both of their feet placed in secure stanchions on the race bike or sulky during the actual race. Drivers must refrain from putting both lines in one hand at any one time in an effort to tap the horse with the whip in the other hand during the stretch to the finish. This again is a safety factor in order to have full control of the horse at all times.

Flack vest

The Trainer and the Training

The trainer has a very important duty in bringing the individual from the sales ring to the first qualifying race. He has to be knowledgeable enough to assess the characteristics of each yearling which are all different and have his grooms made aware of these traits so that they can be treated accordingly. Speaking of grooms, it is an established fact that women are the best in that area. They have that tender-hands approach with softer voices that are all factors in making a fractious young filly or colt learn to trust and obey.

All of the foregoing is very very important before the actual line driving and track training commences. Grooms usually are given duties to look after approximately three individuals. Also, it is essential that each candidate has comfortable, clean, germ free, and safe surroundings as well as *turn-out paddocks* outside where the yearling can feel free to romp, jump, roll, kick up a fuss and get the feeling of freedom which is ingrained in their nature. Often trainers will give a horse a few minutes in the paddock in the morning to let them loosen up and get some early morning kinks out of their 'hept up' system before hitching to the jog cart for serious obedience training by the professional.

Speaking of paddocks, they should be constructed in a way that they are safe in every regard. First the size is very important along with the structure of the walls to be injury-free. Solid wooden posts, planted deeply and firmly approximately 10 feet apart with the material running horizontally being either strong flat lumber or round metal piping and spaced no more than 12 inches apart so that they can't get their heads through. The height should be such that the individual can just put its head over. As to the size, I like about 50 by 50 feet each way and in a square pattern. Do not use electric or metal coils for fencing as serious damage can occur with the possibility of getting a leg through with resultant entanglement. Paddocks should never be long enough to allow a horse to get up too much speed when romping, as on a rainy or wet day they could slide into the structure. Gateways also should be a metal tubing structure with no points where a halter could get caught on or a foot get through. It is important to think proactively so that there are no areas where an injury can occur.

Trailer loading of a horse

Often a lay person may ask a very simple question such as, "How do you get the horse into a trailer, do they not resist?" First of all it is only natural for a young untrained horse to balk at being just being led up a ramp and into the trailer. Every horse person knows this and it is important to take lots of time in doing this for the first time.

Side views of a comfortable, well-ventilated horse trailer. The horse can walk in and walk out.

Fifty percent of the time a well trained horse is very receptive to the normal gentle treatment that it receives daily. When they approach the ramp they often stand and look and if there is already one horse in the trailer it is even more approachable from their viewpoint. The groom or trainer will convey to the subject that they are not going to be hurt in any way. That is a skill. Just the use of a can of grain will entice them to be led forward or just getting their front feet on the ramp will do the job of then going forward with gentle prompting.

If they are hesitant about going forward the most common method is for the leading attendant to tug lightly at the front while at the same time two people join hands around the horse's rear end, pulling it forward. Usually this does the trick and in it goes. Sometimes if they still balk, just covering their eyes with a towel will help.

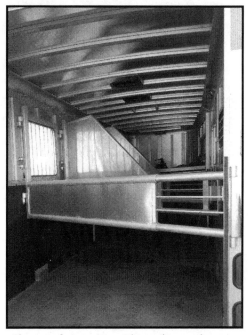

Clean, safe interior with no sharp edges on which the horse could injure itself.

Abusive treatment of any kind is never the right direction to take, although touching them with a whip and then waving it and letting them see it along with the odd loud shout often results in a forward motion. Usually when they have been loaded once or twice it comes naturally after that. Horses on a farm that go to the races weekly will often show excitement at just seeing the sight of a trailer, knowing that this is race day and they can't wait to get loaded. Ninety percent of experienced horses enjoy the competition, contrary to those activists who claim racing to be cruel when in fact the average race horse is far better cared for than the average human.

The Standardbred Horse

The Standardbred horse is so named because long ago when competitive racing began, the rule was that until a Stallion could be called Standardbred, he had to trot a mile in a given time of a mile in two minutes and thirty seconds. Prior to that he was termed non-standard. Likewise the mare was non-standard until such times as her offspring met the two-thirty standard time in trial events.

The standardbred horse races with a so-called *sulky* which is attached to the horse's harness with a quick snap attachment. The harness consists of a backing and brought together with attachments under the belly. It is held forward by a breast strap around the front end and similarly it is held back in position by a so called *crupper* which extends back and under the tail. The bridle or head gear is equipped with various attachments to enhance the horses ability to stay focused at all times. The *bit* is in the mouth and attached on each side to the bridle. Lines are attached to the bit and extend back to the driver so he has control while sitting on the sulky. All of this equipment is kept as light as possible to enhance speed with minimal stress.

When a horse is in training a more durable and heavier vehicle is

Jog cart.

used, called a *jog cart*. It has longer shafts and a more comfortable seating arrangement as hours are spent by the trainer using this vehicle.

In the case of *pacers* they use what is called *hopples* and they more or less are used to keep the rhythm while at high speed. Hopples have a loop at both ends around the legs and then joined together with a strap and held up by straps extending upward and over the back. More recently trotters also use a front leg hopple system to help them maintain the gait at high speed. Since it is imperative to have the horse keep its head directly in front of it when at speed, a long wooden or aluminum rod is attached at the backing of the harness and extends forward to the bridle prohibiting the horse from turning its head sideways. Also attached to a strap under the jaw, or small mini bit in the mouth, is a strap extending up and through the bridle and extending back to a ring on the backing of the harness to hold the horses head up during the racing process and this is called a *check strap*.

Invariably the driver carries a small whip which can be used to touch the horse to encourage more speed but the use of which is kept under very strict control by racing officials. There are at present, discussions that it be eradicated, but in reality it is often a very important instrument to get a horse's attention under very important conditions since the horse knows of its existence and it was essential in keeping a horses attention during its training period. In other words, it is very important when used under proper conditions and under no condition should the whip be used in an abusive manner.

Drivers are a tremendous part of the sport and like in any sport there are *stars* with ingrained abilities far beyond the normal. This fact exists in the horse racing industry. This being so, when one driver consistently is better in every department, it is only normal that owners of horses try to employ their services. At present at any racetrack, there are approximately 15 drivers that are used consistently in all of the races because each of them would, as in any sport, be considered professionals. Younger or beginning drivers, driving at smaller tracks over time will determine who are the best of the best and in time the best will move on to the Class A tracks when openings become available as drivers retire. An outstanding racehorse driver or trainer at the present time is in a very lucrative position in Canadian racing as are the stars in other sports.

Betting on horses

I know from experience that a number of people who make a practice of betting on horses at Canadian tracks, or off-track betting sites, are of the opinion that the owners and trainers have an inside advantage when it comes to making a wager on a given horse such as their own.

Let me inform those people we absolutely depend on their attendance and investments to make our sport viable. It is understood that the track takes out a percentage of the bet, as does the provincial government, plus a percentage goes to the make up of the purses for the given race. This *take out* would collectively amount to approximately 25%. The remaining 75% goes back to the bettor who has correctly selected the winner or proper placings in exotic features in that given race.

The reason that the owner has no advantage is that it is the specific duty of the race secretary who puts the races together to calculate the odds in each race. Sex, speed in last performances, money winnings, age, and several other factors are all considerations in making up those odds a given field.

Winning horses get 50% of the purse, the second horse gets 25%, then 12%, 8%, 5% for the first 5 finishers in the race and the remaining contestants just get the experience of having been in the race.

The majority of owners do not bet on their horses, but are racing for the purse. I have raced horses at various tracks for many years, I bought my first horse in 1952 and have raced continually until this date in 2018 and I definitely abstain from betting on my own horse. Actually I have very little knowledge of where my horse will finish other than HOPE.

The Hambletonian

It has been established that to make real money in the horse racing sport, that you have to invest. The average individual does not have enough available capital to become an owner of the type and breeding necessary to win in the major events where the purse is as much as one million dollars and the winning horse gets 50 %. Year after year the winning horses in these major events have cost the owner in excess of 50 to 100 thousand American dollars at the auctions. Yes, before you read another line you are going to state emphatically, IS THAT SO, well what about so and so that cost nothing near those amounts and went on to beat the world? I will accept those facts as actual but they are few and far between.

At the present time the top money winning trotting sire is Muscle Hill. He commands at very high breeding fee and his offspring are bringing tremendous prices at auction. Why? Because at the race track and at major stakes events he is very often the sire of the winner. Also, of course, just because you pay outrageous dollars for a top bred animal doesn't always bring expected returns at the track. An example is that buyers paid $800,000 for a Muscle Hill colt at Harrisburg in 2016 because he was a full brother to one of sport's greatest trotting fillies. He did not earn $2,000 as a two year old but of course he could still come on and prove his worth.

What is happening now more often, is the trainers are putting together a syndicate of owners, each contributing a share of the purchase price of an individual who has the breeding and confirmation to race against the best. I formed one of the first syndicates back in the 80s when ten people who would not have not have been able, or at least were unwilling if they did have enough money to purchase the individual I had in mind, but collectively we put up enough money to purchase a filly that turned out to be profitable and made in excess of $400.000. One of those individual syndicate owners went forward and invested year after year in horses for himself but watched the more expensive horses being purchased at horse sales winning the races. After that he joined in with small group and now they, after buying the best at the sales, paying the price, are reaping rewards.

There was a time when racing started 250 years ago on the Plains of Abraham, it was the pride of having the fastest horse and people would wager on a winner *Take All* when in a community, the fact of knowing who had the best had to be established. Racing on ice during the winter was a great sport, examples being on the Ottawa River behind Parliament Hill in the 1980s. In 1832 and on the

Rideau Canal, the very first year that the canal filled with water in 1832 and every year thereafter. Now, the sport is big business and the rewards can be very substantial but not always a sure thing. The pride of ownership, and the thrills of winning are considered by many people as being contagious and even losing a bit of money has made the venture very attractive. Again as stated by Winston Churchill, "There is no greater feeling for the inside of a man than the outside of a horse."

Manifestation of My Involvement with Horses

I was born on February 8, 1925 into what was to become a family of six boys and two girls. We lived on a small farm of 100 acres in rural Ottawa and, during the depression years, we, with fantastic parents, enjoyed a great life. As children, we did not know what bad times meant. I recall a one-acre vegetable garden, plenty of hogs, sheep, cows and horses. We interacted with each animal as if it was a part of our family. We also learned early on that the horses were highly valued, and were to be very carefully looked after. They were not food-source animals, but they were essential in enabling us to carry on with our farm work. I hated milking cows, so I was assigned to horse care, plus helping my mom prepare meals.

At the age of 16 I left the farm to join the army.

Aside from the facts as stated above about the horse being part of my upbringing, the very first chance that I got after my military discharge, going back to school, graduating as a Veterinary Surgeon and setting up shop with my wife and family in Shawville, Quebec, I became involved with horses. During my ensuing 52 years in veterinary practice my interest in the care of horses continued to an ever-increasing extent. This interest - and some might say *obsession* - was to become a large part of my life and my future and my family became involved.

Early on I became involved with judging horse shows throughout Ontario and Quebec, including the Ottawa Exhibition and Winter Fair and also the Royal Agricultural Fair in Toronto. As soon as practical I purchased a child-sized pony and got our children all involved in its care and maintenance.

Formerly Brandywine Kid but 'Pete' everyday.

Personally, I also became the proud owner of a Road Horse, a Standardbred Trotter, which is shown hitched to a four-wheeled buggy. In this case quality and speed are invoked, both being shown outside on a track but also inside an arena. Actually, I went through a learning process with different horses with variable successes but it was difficult to find that *top of the line* trotter with lots of stylish front-end action to be judged the winner. One time after having been the judge at a show in Ajax Ontario, and having placed one particular performer at the head of the class, I asked the owner if the said horse was for sale. To make a long story short, I became the owner of this ebony black individual with tremendous personal appearance, brought him home and everywhere that I showed him he was the winner. When the judge came to view our unit, I would only have to call his name "Pete" and he would prune himself with pride.

The Leaves Don't Fall Far From the Tree

It did not take long for my three boys to become associated with their ponies and the duties involved in learning horsemanship. Even though I always kept a man on employ with me to help where needed and to keep a close watch on my horse or horses, we were adamant that the pony or ponies were cleaned daily and fed night, and morning by the young lads.

My middle son Blake with his pony even got a job delivering papers in the village of Shawville and made good pocket money. They showed their pony called 'Spot' hitched to his two-wheeled cart at different fairs when I had time to truck them here and there. One day Blake and younger son Don asked me to take them to the Quyon, Quebec fair but I had a heavy day in veterinary practise so I was unable to take them. When I got back late in the afternoon my wife Mary told me the boys had left on foot for the fair which was 12 miles away.

I immediately took off in search of them and as I entered the fair grounds they were just entering the ring to be judged. As they lined up and the judge came to do his placings of the group 'Spot' proceeded to just lie down as it was his first opportunity to get a rest and he refused to get up. The boys were very disturbed but everyone else had a big laugh, including me, who now had turned my tactics from a disciplinary state to seeing and observing the humour. I did, however, truck them home and they probably didn't need me telling them that they had done the wrong thing.

I think the fair board even gave them a ribbon for their effort. Both they and the pony went to bed early that night without any prompting from me. I have heard them tell that story over and over in later years.

All three boys spent their teen-aged years working as grooms at different race tracks throughout Ontario, Quebec, and even State-side USA. In 1966. My eldest son, Mick, lived and worked in Lexington, Kentucky and wintered in Orlando, Florida working for Canadian and world-renowned trainer and driver, Cecil Champion Stables.

Mick, working in the USA, July, 1966.

I became heavily involved in horse farming in the early 1970s when I moved to my Dunrobin farm in Ontario after practicing Veterinary Medicine in Shawville from 1951 TO 1969. I set up a clinic for surgical treatments and care and Blake, after completing school, became the operations manager.

In 1970 I decided to convert my farm from a series of crop rotations such as barley one year, then corn, then soybeans and so on along with vast numbers of cattle grazing for beef marketing, to the establishment of a horse breeding and training establishment. Some of the areas were considered rather wet and soggy at times so we had approximately 25 of our hundred acres tile drained to alleviate that problem. I selected an area of about

15 acres to build a training track and a new house and a large barn with 12 box stalls in proximity to the track and seeded the rest down to hay cropping. Prior to 1969 we were living in Shawville, Quebec and I had farmed our 100 acres with people hired to do everything.

Speaking of the new house, my whole family of three boys and one girl were with my wife and me so we built one large enough with four bedrooms to make sure there was lots of room. At this same time we planted several trees as the whole area near the house was rather barren in appearance.

Now about the training track, I had surveyor come and plan the lay out so that the turns were elevated and the straight ways properly graded, the whole thing being just short of a half mile in circumference and surfaced with stone dust.

The house with the track in front.

Then training began with a hired head trainer and a few grooms along with all my boys getting involved on a very part time basis at the same time along with their formal schooling. They were also picking up all the tricks of the trade so to speak. We had a few yearlings of our own along with most of the rest owned by paying outsiders.

It is amazing now in 2018 to think back to those times when all roads in the area were still gravel surfaced in all directions and traffic was very minimal. This being the case, when the track conditions were not optimal, they would take two or three horses at a time and train on the roads with very few problems with cars as most owners were local and gave way to the horses when any problem existed or presented itself. Then of course time marches on, more people came to live in our beautiful area with the Ottawa River and views of the Gatineau Hills being an attraction and the roads were paved. Consequently that practice of training on the roads became a *no no*, as it was not safe for horse or man.

Since my boys were all revved up about the horse business, I was anxious to keep them working. I also encouraged them move on during the summer holidays and work with other stables in the Toronto racing areas and the oldest boy even worked in the United States.

We set up a horse training stable with some eight to ten grooms and trainers and called the company 'Armstead Farms.' We also expanded into a horse breeding stable. We stood two or three stallions which included the purchase of a top stallion from Hanover Shoe farms in Pennsylvania and mares from all over Ontario were coming to be bred. This also meant the building of a lean-to the big barn to house the incoming mares. Our training establishment was running well and actually at a point where we were turning applications for training away as our business was considered very effective in the racing world.

At one point there were as many as 70 mares and racing recruits on the farm at one time. I carried out a full-fledged practice at the same time and spent most of my time on the road doing calls but all with horses.

My son Blake, now in his late 20s was the farm manager and along with all his duties, was in control of the breeding of the mares artificially. This meant that semen was collected from the sire and the mares were bred with use of manual introduction of the semen into the uterus of the mare when, after scientific examination, had proven to be in a receptive stage of ovulation it was time to be bred. This method was carried out because the semen from one ejaculation of the sire could be diluted and used to breed several mares on the same day, where the sire on such a given day, would otherwise not be able to breed so many mares naturally.

Every year I had senior student from the Veterinary College at my place during the summer where they studied on the job and were a tremendous help for me. All of this operation was going on at the farm when I at the same time was managing the Rideau Carleton Raceway and practicing veterinary medicine. From 1975 to 1980 I also became very much involved in the management of the racing industry serving as President of both the Canadian Standardbred Horse Society, the breeding portion, and President of the Canadian Trotting Association, the governing body of racing in Canada. Following that I took over management of the Rideau Carleton Raceway in 1980.

Everything was humming along at a very lucrative level when a major disaster occurred in our family bringing the whole operation to a screeching halt. At 27 years of age Blake, my irreplacable son and head of everything, lost his life in a vehicle-oriented accident.

He had been working on making his antique car turn into a model *beauty*. Unfortunately, on August 21 in 1981, he was taking it on a trial run. The car had no muffler and carbon monoxide leaked into the car which resulted in poisoning him.

He was deeply admired and loved. He and his beautiful wife had just moved into a new house which he constructed himself from pine logs that he cut from a local bush. One can only understand the devastating effect it had on his wife and our whole family and, of course, the whole farming endeavour. The results of this disaster brought about the complete disbanding of our horse business and all that remained was the training of horses which continued under a special arrangement but not under my control or interest.

My son Don remained attached to and interested in the racing fraternity and worked on the farm with trainers of young horses. In the summer after school was over he continued working with noted stables in Toronto and one day when it came time to go back to school to further his high school towards obtaining his matriculation, he informed me he was a not coming back home to go to school. He and I had a little discussion and while he was over 16 and had the right to quit school as far as government regulations were concerned, he still had to deal with me. As a bribe I promised that if he would continue to get his grade 12 that I would buy him a yearling filly at Harrisburg and he agreed.

I kept my promise and he returned home and went back to school. The filly I bought him, called *Belle Bluecrest*, was trained by him and was very successful winning major stakes for him. He then became a driver and raced all my candidates plus several others. He later got involved in the Racing industry and for two years became a junior judge at several tracks. Then girls came into his life and he decided to come home.

I advised him to leave the sport as a full-time occupation but to continue in it as a hobby while seeking permanent employment which would provide him with a pension in view of retirement down the road. He got a job in the city of Ottawa and worked there for more than 30 years but always kept his interest in racing on the side. He eventually married and raised three girls.

As for me, following our son Blake's death my wife Mary became ill. I sold the 50 acres with the racing stables and house, moved over to the remaining 50 acres and built another house - a bungalow which was better for Mary during her illness. Unfortunately Mary passed away in 1985. Time passed and I remarried again and in 2013, after 23 good years, cancer brought the end to that marriage.

The bungalow.

Now my son Don decided it was time to get back into racing and training full time again so he retired from the City of Ottawa. At that time the original farm of 50 acres that I had sold back in the 80s came up for sale and Don bought it back and now in 2018 he is back training young horses full time for me, himself and others.

We had several people interested in racing and owning a horse but found the whole thing rather expensive so I once again opened up a public syndicated ownership environment and eventually got 10 people to invest $5,000 each to develop a pot of $50,000 from which I bought a filly at the London Ontario sales for $27,000 and it is now in training on the farm with Don.

From day one, after this filly arrived home from the sale she was a so-called "HAND FULL." The very first lesson is to be tied to a post with a simple loop around the neck that does not choke them if they resist and fly back. It is an important lesson to have them stand at your command so that that they can be handled for brushing and grooming. Previously at the breeding farm where they would be getting ready for the sale there would more than one person around them to get them looked after.

Beginning lesson one, we tied the filly to a post in the middle of our paddock. This filly resisted *big time* and pulled backward so hard that she fought it and fought it until she threw herself down and squealed with disapproval. As she lay there on the ground, we watched to ensure that she was not choking or otherwise hurting herself. We just left her there until she decided that this was not for her. After about five minutes, she got up and stood for a few minutes assessing the situation. Then she tried a strong pull again and struggled on the line for a bit but did not go down.

That was her last attempt at being the boss and she began to submit to our gentle touching, rubbing and being sociable to the point that now she does everything we ask on command.

She had to learn about having her feet picked up for cleaning in preparation for the future application of shoes and normal body cleaning. Horses as a whole are very intelligent and are creatures of habit. They usually learn quite quickly that you are in command and they want to be receptive and cooperative. The most important thing for the trainer to do is to obtain that important liaison.

Eventually the process of harnessing was introduced.

One has to understand that the putting on of the harness is a traumatic experience for a horse, so this has to be done gradually. The horse has to have the opportunity to become comfortable with each stage before the next stage is introduced.

First the trainer takes the harness and lets the equine smell it and become familiar with it. He/she then moves to the back of the animal and rubs it a few times before putting the belly band part on its back with the ends hanging down on both sides for future fastening underneath. Nothing has been tightened yet.

All harness has to be securely held in place during racing, so a chest strap is put in place and attached to keep the harness from moving backward. The harness is kept from moving forward by a strap running from the backing of the harness to the tail where the strap goes under the tail in a loop. This loop is called the crupper. These procedures hold the harness in place. All is well now and we tighten the belly band and attach the cart and training can begin.

After getting the horse harnessed and hitched to the cart the last item on the harness to note is the part that ensures that the horse's head is at the right elevation and pointed in the right direction. This done by having a strap that runs from a second *or mini* bit that is placed in the mouth in addition to the driving bit. This mini bit is attached on each side of the mouth to a strap that joins to a single strap that runs up the face and over the top of the head and back to a hitch on the top of the main harness. This firm strap is variable in length depending on how high the trainer wants the head elevated. The main strap is called a *Check*.

The purpose in keeping the horses head high in front helps the flow of air as it is breathed directly into the lungs. To assist in keeping the head directly in front many trainers use a *head pole*, which is telescopic in nature as it slides in and out. It is attached to the back pad of the harness, runs forward and is attached to the bridle at the mouth level. Also, I might add that, in place of a mini bit in the mouth, the strap often just runs around under the lower jaws in a comfortable loop and joins again on the front of the face half way between the nostrils and the eyes.

Usually the trainer carries small delicate 'whip' to use if attention is being disregarded by the horse during its period of training. Often a little tap on the hip will bring the horse's attention back to the trainer.

After the addition of the harness for the first few days the trainers *line drives* them in the paddock where they are going alone without a cart and are taught to *stop, go, turn right* or *left* with a slight tug on the line attached to the mouth bit. The command 'Gee' is given for right turn and 'Haw' for left, 'Woo' for stop, and a click sound from the driver's mouth to request a forward motion. After a few days doing this they are then hitched to the jog cart and with one extra person with a long line attached to the bit, sits on the side of the cart with the driver to help prevent a runaway should the horse get excited during their early lessons.

Usually the colt or filly is given the day off with the trainer on Sunday but should they miss a day during the week due to weather or whatever, then they will often fill in the training schedule by going on Sunday. The distance for jogging increases weekly starting at one or two miles per day and up to six miles by the third month.

As for speed, this is not a concern until they have learned all their steering lessons. Then *interval training* for speed is used. If the training starts in October or November by the end of January they could be up to a three-minute mile which can be increased by ten seconds monthly until race time in May or June when they must show that they are up to a mile at a given declared speed before the judges who will time you. When you have attained the qualifying speed it is off to the races or stakes.

Donnie putting WarraweeUTO through her daily juvenile training.
Photo by Bob Webster

We, who train yearlings in Canada and stay here year round, of course are subjected to varying training track conditions with respect to weather. Many eastern Canadians go to Florida or South

Carolina each year during the winter months, or in Western Canada trainers may go to California. Over the past many years the actual benefits regarding the south have been questioned as, in many cases, it has been proven that horses trained in Canada have raced just as well as those trained under more pleasant conditions in the south.

Horses trained under winter conditions in Canada, because of snow, ice wind, cold temperatures, shoes having to have points welded onto their surface to prevent slipping, and so on, have been prepared better than those trained in the south when it comes to variable track conditions such as rain and mud in the summer. The horses trained in Canada have been subjected to those many variables on a regular basis and have learned to adapt so rain and mud can easily be *taken in stride.*

There is, however, no comparison when it comes to the comfort of the trainer in respect to the two variables. Having noted all of the comments above, in the final analysis it boils down to what areas for training are the best economically and desired by the owner and trainer. Personally, I envy those training in the south, as does my son Don himself, who during his early days as a summer student, spent time with trainers in the south wearing a tee shirt and shorts and sun glasses and loved it. Now in Dunrobin, Ontario, where he trains, it calls for mitts, scarf, fleece-lined underwear, big felt-lined boots and socks his grandmother knitted, face mask, goggles and two cups of hot coffee between training runs. But, regardless of the weather conditions and the hardship involved, he says that he is *'living his dream.'* Such is his love for horses and horsemanship.

Acquiring a Possible Champion

In the Standardbred racing world almost all young horses, especially yearlings, are sold and purchased at sales set up by the racing industry. The odd sale however may be done privately but that is very unusual. For instance, Standardbred Canada's publicity department has a sales section which will set a date, preferably in late October, to hold the sale at a specific location. Breeders are then invited to submit their candidates to be listed for sale in a catalogue which will be distributed to known buyers and trainers well in advance so that potential buyers can scan the entrees of both pacers and trotters with the objective of choosing potential champions.

Having done this they will proceed to the sale and examine their possible purchases for confirmation and suitability. Here is where the decisions are really made. Most buyers know after examination of the pedigrees the assets of the yearling that they are considering, and in what range the actual sale price will be. This in itself determines which horse they will bid on as the price will be an important determining factor.

Prior to entering the ring for sale, the auctioneer will read off the assets of each and every yearling. All the good points of the individual are spelled out as well as the past performance of the sire and dam (mother and father) plus the offspring of the dam and how well they have done on the track re speed and money earned.

Then the bidding starts and the last person to bid becomes the owner. It is also clearly explained in the catalogue, in large print, that the owner is the owner when the sales hammer is cracked down with the auctioneers loud word 'SOLD.' This means that there is no *come back* re the soundness or defects of the individual. It is taken for granted that you the buyer did all this examination beforehand.

Characteristics of a Champion

I would like now to move to the actual inspections that are done beforehand. Many people who are potential owners are in the sport because of their acquired love of the sport and all the excitement therein but are not in the position nor do they have the ability to examine the qualities in regards to the confirmation and characteristics required to be a top equine athlete. These prospective owners will then employ certain people who have that proven ability to do so and, in many instances, even leave it up to them to do the bidding. Once the decision has been made between the owner and the examiner regarding their potential purchase, is where the experience and knowledge comes into affect. When making confirmation decisions and so on, there are many established requirements. The examiner will check first the horse as to its general attitude and manners. Does it have the correct size, height, softness of the eye and width of forehead, size of the nostrils, width of the jaws to enhance breathing. How does it stand? Are the front legs straight with proper distance apart with prominent chest muscles and a sloping shoulder, with a good spring of ribs to allow deep breathing? The knees should be flat and mature and not set back. The hind legs also should be set under them in a straight manner and not be so called *sickle hocked* or *bowed*.

Finally the most important point of all is the feet, which have to be the proper size and description to carry the speed and function which will be required of them. There is an old saying, "No foot, no horse."

The same overall qualities of a yearling apply regardless of sex but examination of genital areas all play a part as some day they may be moved to the breeding ranks if they have proven themselves on the track. The better they have performed on the track the more sought after they will be as sires or dams of the next generation of champions.

Everything I have said regarding what to look for is only a small guide to ending up with the right horse who will stand the rigours of approximately nine months of training by a competent individual. Then it comes to the day when it must meet a certain standard of speed and ability in a specific qualifying race before competent horse judges.

Bloodlines

It is an established fact that we horse people spend endless hours doing in-depth studies into certain blood lines we like and dislike when we are choosing which stallion we should breed our very valuable mare to or visa versa when breeding farms have a very important sire available and far more than one hundred mares have been nominated to be served by that stallion.

The breeding consultant on the farm spends many, many hours looking into bloodlines regarding speed and money earned and other outstanding qualities before informing said applicants which mares he is accepting.

I state the following aside humorously, yes please remember I said 'humorously,' but I am also sure we horse people often spend much less time checking into the bloodlines of a member of the opposite sex that we have fallen deeply in love with. Their looks and other superficial qualities may have been of paramount concern before we asked them to spend the rest of their lives with us with the hopes of raising a family. Furthermore, the bloodlines of the suitor may also have not been of prime concern when the proposal was accepted.

Now back again when talking of bloodlines, the word 'bloodlines' means much more than just factors like speed and money earnings. Attributes such as confirmation is often considered if your mare say has certain faults such as size and so on and you will look for a sire to correct this flaw in the proposed offspring. Certain crosses in bloodlines have been established for many reasons. For example, a lot of people want a cross of *Valley Victory* to be in the back records of both sire and dam in a proposed future trotting prospect, and these established facts go on and on. I accent the word **back** in the breeding lines because at the same time you don't want a ridiculous cross by breeding a *MuscleMass* mare to her sire. This close breeding often results in the worst qualities of the sire coming out in the offspring and seldom the best factors.

Breeding

Regarding artificial breeding of horses let me be more specific. Today when any given race horse has been spectacular in its racing career and also has a fantastic breeding background regarding its dam and sire it is often brought into the breeding side of the industry. Since it obviously is worth a lot of money, it is often sold for a great sum in the way of shares.

Each share-holder, we will say, gets one or more servicings from the sire using mares from his or her ownership or they can be sold privately to some one else. The sire often starts out at a modest breeding fee but it can become very lucrative for the share-holders if the resultant offspring do well on the racetrack regarding speed and money earned. Since the industry limits the number of breedings to 100 per season per sire and the fact that many mares may have be bred on the same day, the semen is collected and a fluid base is used to increase the volume available to be inseminated on that given day. All mares in the breeding shed are examined daily and are encouraged to arrive at their ovulation date by teasing them with a stallion kept for that purpose who will be under control as it smells and her vulva and the lifting of her tail with small urinations.

She will then be manually examined by the veterinarian who will often do a rectal examination and feel the ovaries to ensure a follicle thereon is ready to ovulate. The semen is collected by having an artificial structure covered with a soft blanket surface to resemble a mare and contaminated with the urine from a mare ready for breeding which has a *come-on* odour for the stallion. When he rises to breed the so-called decoy, the agent has an artificial rubber vagina which is so designed with body temperature water surrounding the vagina part. This apparatus is held with his left hand as he grasps the erect penis with his right hand and guides it into the rubber vagina which has a flask on the end to collect the semen upon ejaculation.

This semen is then taken to the office and kept under sterile and temperature-wise conditions while the diluent is added to enhance the volume. Then it is divided into portions to breed various mares. In this way many mares can be bred by the same stallion on any given day which would be impossible under natural breeding conditions. An added advantage is that the stallion is in much less danger of being kicked by an unwelcoming mare.

Breeding by Artificial Means

Drugs

Further to the act of artificial breeding, if the mare is brought to heat by means of using drugs that stimulate ovulation there is always the possibility of causing super ovulation meaning more than one egg or ova is produced, resulting in twins, which no one wants. It is much better to let them ovulate naturally which occurs mostly in the spring months.

Roly Armitage

Controlling Ovulation

Ovulation comes about naturally stimulated by the length of daylight hours and nature wants the foal to be born on the pasture in May with its green grass and beautiful weather. The longest days are in June and breeding then would result in having a green-grass foal eleven months later in May.

The length of day from a visual aspect can be enhanced by lengthening the daylight artificially. This is done by simply leaving the lights on for a few extra hours in the mare's stall well after normal *lights-out* in the evenings thus stimulating ovulation so breeding can occur earlier than normal. The resultant foal will be that much older as the objective is to have the foal born as close to the beginning of January as possible.

Embyro Transfer

A situation may exist where a champion mare has literally torn all the racing records apart and upon her retirement she goes to the breeding shed to reproduce herself and, hopefully, her racing records. After a proper stallion is selected to be her *boyfriend*, so to speak, the problem may be that the mare is not physically or otherwise in a condition to have an offspring.

Having accepted this fact, when the mare comes into heat she can be bred artificially or otherwise to a stallion which has been selected to be the sire. Upon conception an embryo is produced which travels its way down the fallopian tube to be embedded on the wall of her uterus. This embryo is then flushed manually from her uterus after about the seventh day and it is then transferred to a host or surrogate mare which has been prepared for conception.

That embryo transfer results in a live foal eleven months later. The foal has all the genes and characteristics of the original donors and the host mare has no influence on the offspring other than being the host. This procedure can also be done to a very physically normal champion mare which allows her to produce a foal and still continue on with her racing career.

Date of Birth

All horses are considered to have their date of birth on the 1st of January following their birth. All this is done because we race fillies or colts at two years of age, many in the Ontario Sires Stakes program, starting about June or July and therefore a foal born in February the previous year, would have a decided advantage over a foal born in May or June. Personally I, and several others, are opposed to racing these two-year-old *babies* as they are months away from maturity but the high costs involved in getting them from conception to the races dictates that we try to get our cost of investment returned as soon as possible. However, having said that, from a Veterinary standpoint the care and love extended to these horses is very humane and in any case only a small number from the total born in a given year do make it to the races as two-year-olds and the majority are held over to race as three-year-olds or older when, of course, they are more mature.

Barnyard Surgery

During the time I was looking after the horses in the bush operations there was often a problem with getting sufficient numbers of good workhorses. In order to fill that need a company arranged to have carloads of stallion horses come from the western provinces to northern Quebec, many of them still wild and unbroken with long manes and tails - actually outlaws in a sense. They would be unloaded into a corral at the railway sidings and then trucked and put together in a large barn where they would be in a herd, watered and fed.

Those stallions would not have had a human hand put on them from the time they were rounded up in the west until they were in the large shed and I was presented with the job of castrating them. This was done in order to make them more amenable to breaking, that is *trained* and being made ready to draw logs.

When the day came I would have a horseman or my veterinary assistant, in a loft above the horses. He would drop down a 'lasso' which is a rope with loop to go around the horse's neck. Then we had to get the horse out of the door below and let it run out to where I was with the other end of the long rope. With the help of one or two men we would wrap it around a tree nearby. As the horse was pulling from the attached tree I would inject succinal choline, a sedative, into the enlarged neck vein which would cause immediate paralysis and during this five minute period I would convert the stallion into a gelding and then release it from the lasso which was rigged with a quick release mechanism.

This would go on until the whole carload of horses had been subjects of my rather crude but effective surgery. The horses would then be herded into a barn nearby and would then be directed into a chute or box the size of the animal and secured there as each foot would then be pulled up forcefully by a winch-type device and its feet would be trimmed and steel shoes put on both front feet. This horse would then be paired with a very quiet old campaigner gelding or mare and hitched to a flat stone boat-type sleigh and out they would go so it would learn its job of being a workhorse. The quiet old horse would not allow a runaway to happen and this method of training would go on until each new arrival got the message that its job was to pull logs.

Preventable Diseases and Conditions

There are several diseases that horses can be subjected to in different parts of the world but in Canada we limit vaccinations normally to prevent **Tetanus** which is a condition which can be readily contracted via any wound. It can also be called 'lock jaw' because of its muscle contraction nature and for all intents and purposes is considered essential in our vaccination program as it is lethal.

Likewise we vaccinate against **Rabies** which of course is a death-causing agent, although at this point it has almost been eradicated. Even in the wild life it is very rare as the government drops an edible oral vaccine from an aircraft in all wooded areas. The disease for horses comes as the result of a bite from in infected animal.

Since **Influenza** outbreaks are quite common at tracks where horses congregate, or even at training establishments, we make it a point to vaccinate horses against this problem. At least in the horse's early years, but they have a tendency to become more immune as they get older.

All race horses are mandatorily subjected to a blood test called **'The Coggins Test'** on an annual basis. This is a test for **Infectious Anemia**, which is transferred from infected horses by way of the mosquito bite and is incurable. It is also called **Swamp Fever** because originally it was found to be more prevalent in swampy areas or districts where the mosquito problem would be more abundant. Again at this point due to the annual testing and so forth the disease has almost become non-existent.

Another very important management aspect regarding a horses health is the **worming problem**. Horses have a habit of picking up worm eggs from infected neighbouring horses resulting in worms hatching in the their intestines, accumulating to the point of causing colic (gut pain) or numbers of the eggs can accumulative to the point of causing blockage of the bowel. Mostly however their main problem is resultant anemia due to one species of worms being blood suckers. Horsemen now treat for worm prevention on an ongoing basis with a series of oral treatments using drugs that are very specific and effective.

Getting back to the subject of **infectious anemia** or **swamp fever**. I personally recall when I was checking horses going into the lumber camps back in the 50s for this disease and in one area of western Quebec it was so prevalent that I had no option but to test and euthanize several positive carriers to prevent the spread of the disease to incoming horses from clean areas, especially, the car loads coming in from dry areas of western Canada where there was no disease. At that point there was no scientific test such as the *Coggins Test* which was found and developed by a Dr. Coggins, who was also a veterinarian. Consequently, my test at that point was to take about twenty cubic centimetres of blood and subject the said sample to a centrifuge which would separate the blood cells in the sample from the *serra* (liquid part) and if the percentage of blood cells were significantly lower than normal, that horse was immediately put down.

Buying That Special One and Possible Pitfalls

Being a veterinarian, I was involved early in the treating of sick and injured horses along with yearly vaccinations and minor surgery and so on. Consequently, I caught the so-called BUG of horse ownership disease and wanted to get involved in racing. I did buy and train several yearlings with reasonable break-even success.

One time I thought *I am going to buy a future champion*, while realizing that it would cost a lot of money. There was this horse which was setting the world on fire at several tracks and his half-brother was in the sale at Harrisburg, Pennsylvania, a reputable sale that has been going on for years where the champions are sold. I went to the sale and when I went to examine my candidate, the owner driver and trainer of the half brother champion were there examining this particular horse for possible ownership. They spent a lot of time trotting it back and forth and so on and then walked away. I stepped up and did all the necessary checks: to my eye he appeared excellent in every way except his feet were rather small and contracted a bit.

I observed the next day at the sale that the original people were not bidding but several other people were. I thought I would take the chance regardless of its feet to buy him and although I expected the price to be in the $30,000 league, I bought him for $21,000, this being in 1970s when a dollar was a dollar so to speak. I brought him home and he showed all the class during training that was expected of a future champion. He qualified right on schedule and won his early races and my son, the trainer, was very enthusiastic about him. He raced him at Montreal's Blue Bonnets Race Track and he won three races in a row and every body was talking and I was pleased of course that I had bought it in spite of the original people who owned his champion brother having decided to pass on his purchase.

Shortly after his performance in Montreal. I got a call from someone asking me if I would sell with an offer of $70,000. I talked it over with my son and refused the offer. Not more than a week later the horse came up lame in those same small feet and never raced again. I sold him to another man who thought he could fix the problem for the nominal sum of $5,000. I learned early that there are several hills and valleys in the racing industry as there are in all sports or endeavours. Oh! Don't feel sorry for me because I once bought a yearling at a sale for

$14,000 and as a two and three year old in the Ontario Sires Stakes, made $220,000 and then sold it State Side for $35,000. The old saying, 'Some you win. Some you lose,' certainly rings true in the sport of horse racing.

One of my many stories - Best Intentions

I was in Harrisburg, Pennsylvania at their annual mixed horse sales. When I say *mixed* it means all types of horses, but the dates categorize them by selling yearlings one day, brood mares another day and race horses on still another day.

On one occasion this very well-bred yearling filly called 'Best Intentions' was up for sale and but her dam was a twin which everyone shies away from. She was going for a low price but I took a chance and bought her for $6000 which was a steal.

I brought her home and she was not in training very long before she was showing all the qualities of a future champion. There, however, was one problem and that was that she was not eligible to enter any major stake races where she could make much money for me. I knew that there was one area where she would do well and that was in Quebec which had a series of races for two-year-old fillies, but it was for Quebec residents only. The filly had to be owned in Quebec on January 1st of the year of racing.

I saw this as a chance for this exceptional filly to make a name for herself, so I went to a friend of mine in Quebec and said to him, "Give me $6000 for my filly and you can race her, pay all the bills and so on and take any money she earns BUT at the end of the series I have the right to buy her back for the same $6000, with the understanding that her value would be high because of her expected accomplishments. He agreed to the deal and gave me cheque dated January 1st of that year. Now he was the owner of an eligible filly for the stakes which were high.

The filly raced in Montreal, Three Rivers, and Quebec City and just ran away as a winner in all races. The new owner, as well as myself, was delighted. Following one race one of the competitors who we had been beaten in all events so far, appealed to the Quebec Racing Commission on the technicality that the filly was not eligible to race in the stakes because she was not owned by a Quebec owner prior to January 1st. He stated that the filly should have been the property of the new owner on December 31 so she would be Quebec owned on the first of Jan 1st to qualify with the January 1st stipulation.

The new owner appealed and at a meeting of all involved, the commission ruled that the cheque issued on January 1st had not been cashed on time to make it eligible and the filly was there and then disqualified and all monies had to be returned and redistributed to the others who were defeated in the races. I bought the filly back as previously agreed upon.

It didn't stop there. At the same time I was a candidate to become the president and head of racing in Canada and all was in order for the election to take place. At the meeting in Toronto my opponent brought up the subject about my involvement in the event in Quebec and said there were those who were saying that when I had made a deal with my friend in Quebec just to make the filly eligible it made them question my integrity and honesty. I immediately said to the electorate there that I did not want even one vote from anyone if they felt for one minute that there were hidden clauses in the dealing of the horse going to Quebec.

Fortunately one of the members from the Quebec commission was also a director of the Canadian Racing organization and I turned to him and said, "Sir, you were on the board who made my filly ineligible due to the date problem but even you said at the meeting that I was totally exonerated from any dishonesty." Then he stood up and spoke very highly regarding my unquestionable honesty and integrity in the whole matter. I was elected thereafter by a huge majority as President of the Canadian Trotting Association.

Best Intentions went on for me to be an outstanding race mare and was second in three races against the filly of the year named 'Handle with Care' who that year was undefeated in any of her starts and was named the most outstanding filly in both Canada and United States winning the prestigious award 'Two Year Old Filly of The Year.'

The Horse and the Lumbering Industry

In the area about the use of the horse, aside from the well-established facts relating to the history of man and beast opening the wilderness of Canada, I personally was involved in the logging industry in Northern Quebec from 1951 to 1964.

There were seven different companies involved in the timber trade and the draft horse was involved in bringing the logs down from the regional mountainous areas to the surrounding lakes. These lakes would be damned up until the spring run off took place. My duties as a veterinarian were to oversee the care and health maintenance of all the horses on a regular or urgent basis.

At least once a week I would fly by chartered aircraft from the Ottawa River base in a small plane piloted by WW2 Canadian Air Force veteran Iverson Harris to the lumber camps. We landed on the various frozen lakes near where the horses were stabled and under the care of an experienced caretaker.

At any given time there would be 500 horses in the different camps with almost that many in reserve. Most, but not all, of the horses were owned by and leased from surrounding farmers who used these animals in their farm operations in the summer and fall and then they would lease them to the bush operations. The horses would all be vaccinated against Tetanus Rabies and influenza as well as being dewormed annually. The animals were also examined for minor cuts and bruises.

Rabies first became evident in Canada during the late 18th and early 19th centuries. However, only a few sporadic outbreaks, mainly in domestic animals, were noted before 1945.

In the early 19th century - in 1818 - The Duke of Richmond [1] was appointed Governor General of British North America and during the summer of 1819 he undertook an extensive tour of Upper and Lower Canada. While in Sorel, Quebec he was bitten on the hand by a fox. The injury apparently healed, and he continued to York (Toronto) and Niagara (Niagara-on-the-Lake, Ont.), even examining military sites as far distant as Drummond Island. Returning to Kingston, he planned a leisurely visit to the settlements on the Rideau. During this part of the journey the first symptoms of hydrophobia [2]

---

[1] https://richmondvillage.ca/our-village/history-of-richmond/

[2] Early symptoms can include fever and tingling at the site of exposure. These symptoms are followed by one or more of the following symptoms: violent movements, uncontrolled excitement, fear of water, an inability to move parts of the body, confusion, and loss of consciousness. Once symptoms appear, the result is nearly always death. The time period between contracting the disease and the start of symptoms is usually one to three months; however, this time period can vary from less than one week

appeared. The disease developed rapidly and on the 28th of August he died in extreme agony in a barn a few miles from a settlement that had been named in his honour.

The night before his death, he slept at the "Masonic Arms", which was renamed the "Duke of Richmond Arms" to commemorate the visit.

Rabies in foxes spread into the Canadian provinces from the Arctic regions during the late 1940s. The disease gradually died out in most areas and was not considered a major concern.

I diagnosed the first case of rabies in the northern part of Quebec while attending to the horses at one of the lumber camps at John Bull. It was a special call to the camp because one particular horse was acting strangely. Upon arrival the horse was walking in circles in a rather blind state and finally threw itself down and was more or less paralyzed. I had never seen anything like that before but since rabies had always been in the Arctic Fox we expected that at any time it could migrate south into the populated areas of Canada. This geographical point was as close to the north as anywhere else so I suspected rabies. I warned everyone to stay clear as the saliva is virulent and for the proper diagnosis pathologically the animal had to die of the disease so I ordered that it was not to be euthanized.

---

to more than one year. The time is dependent on the distance the virus must travel along <u>nerves</u> to reach the <u>central nervous system</u>.

I came home and called the authorities in Ottawa and their immediate response to me was, "It Can't be Rabies because there is none below the Arctic Circle." I responded, "But I think there is now and since this a reportable disease, you must fly in to remove the head."

They reluctantly came to Shawville, Que, flew in to the camp, picked up the head and in the Ottawa laboratory the result was proven positive for Rabies and alarm was sounded across the whole country to start vaccinations against rabies big time.

Okay, back to the lumber business.

On occasion there were major injuries to deal with. The logs would be manufactured on site by the many men who would be billeted in lumber camps. Those men worked very hard and lived in very primitive conditions. In the sleeping quarters there were long rows of beds and a central box stove to generate heat. The hygienic facilities were an outside toilet except for the washrooms which were at one end of the shanty or sleeping quarters. The dining areas were very adjacent to the central sleeping quarters and food was good, wholesome and plentiful. The basics were meat, potatoes, carrots or turnip, oceans of bread, butter jam, and desserts of all kinds baked on site. Everything was presented in bowls and if you wanted more all you did was point at the dish you wanted and down it came to you as absolutely no speaking was allowed at the table. It was 'Shut up and eat, then get out and let the *Cookie* get the place cleaned up."

Most of the men came up in the fall and stayed until the spring drive only going home for Christmas.

The operation consisted of a single horse drawing a log all the way down to the lake alone. Then it was unhitched there on the lake, given a mouth full of grain or a drink and the same horse on its own, they being creatures of habit and training, would go back to from whence it started. If a young horse was reluctant to make the return trip, the horse would be hooked to the tail of an obliging horse and off they went.

When all the logs were on the ice and spring had arrived and the Colounge River was full flowing, the damned lakes would be opened. The flowing water, the aforementioned *drive,* sent the logs down to Davidson and Fort Colounge.

This River Drive was a massive operation in itself where many men with caulked boots would actually walk over the logs and with a 'Pike Pole' which was a long stick or pole with a spiked end to stick into and push a jammed log on its way. Sometimes if a large number of logs piled up causing a jam, they would use dynamite charges to get them on their way.

Each log was stamped on the end to identify which company owned which log, and when on their arrival in the Ottawa River they would be collected and sent by rafts to the respective owners, Gillies Lumber in Arnprior, Ontario being one of the largest companies along with Boyle in Davidson, Quebec where they were sawed into lumber in their large sawmills. Consolidated Paper had their logs collected into booms which is a large pod of floating logs all held together with a series of large logs held together with loops of chain. These booms would be towed by steam barges down the Ottawa River. [3]

An amusing and interesting event occurred when one my sons was at our cottage on the river. He would not go to bed until the nightly boom of logs would be steaming slowly by. Then he would flash his large light out to the tug boat and the very obliging captain would pull the rope on his fog horn 'Hoot, Hoot' and my boy would then happily go to bed. Some years later I met the very obliging captain of that particular barge and we had a good laugh.

---

[3]

https://www.google.ca/search?q=lumber+camps+in+canada&source=lnms&tbm=isch&sa=X&ved=0ahUKEwjSxZ_Ts4_ZAhWG7YMKHWolAUMQ_AUICigB&biw=1250&bih=612#imgrc=sHSY6xiRqbqYtM:

Horses at War

Everyone knows that there are trillions of variables that have to occur for you, the individual, to ever present yourself to live on this earth. My father was 35 years old which is really old for a soldier to join the armed forces. Nevertheless when war broke out in 1914, he was one of many men who answered the call for Canada to join with Britain and the Commonwealth to defend our way of life against Germany, the aggressor.

There was an outstanding man - Colonel Sam Hughes then head of militia in Canada and stationed in Ottawa under the direction of Major General Sir Edward Morrison who directed Hughes to put together the First Canadian Division of some 32,000 men which were assembled from across Canada and sent for training at Val Cartier in Quebec.

Along with the men were the same number of horses. My father was one of those men. After intensive training Hughes had assembled some 30 ships of various sizes to come to the port of Quebec. Meanwhile the men and horses marched all the way from Val Cartier to Quebec and became seaborne on a convoy to England.

On arrival they were sent to Salisbury plains in the south of England. They trained there for a year under very adverse conditions of continuous rain and mud; housed only in tents. My father was a gunner in the Canadian Artillery portion of the army.

Early in 1915 they broke camp and loaded into ships and arrived in France, then on to the Belgium area of Ypres and Vimy in the spring. In the early months of the war between them and the German forces in the heat of battle the Germans sent over a yellow cloud of mustard gas[4] which was definitely outlawed by United Nations regarding acts of war.

My dad, confronted with this, took out his handkerchief, wet it with his own urine and held it front of his face, as did the others. They also got down as close to the ground as possible to be out of the drift. He survived this attack and after a few days behind the lines and a week of coughing he was sent forward with a horse and flat-bottomed boat[5] loaded with shells. He proceeded forward in the mud; walking under those conditions made it necessary for him to ride the horse. He proceeded to the gun area to deliver the shells. At this very point a German artillery shell landed right in front of them,

---

[4] http://ww1.canada.com/battlefront/the-first-poison-gas-attack-in-1915-at-ypres
The first Canadians who had to deal with chemical weapons -- the soldiers of the First Canadian Division in the second battle of Ypres on April 22-24, 1915. The Canadians had the bad luck to be situated smack dab in the middle of the first *poison gas* attack in history.

[5] In Canada this was called a stoneboat - a contraption without wheels which was used to transport stones out of the fields as the land was being cleared. In battle situations when the land was very wet wheels would have become mired in the mud.

killing the horse he was riding on. The horse fell back on him and the saddle horn penetrated his abdomen leaving him in critical condition and open to infection. Furthermore, the concussion from blast left him with massive hearing loss.

He was picked up by medics and transferred to the first aid post and due to the seriousness of wound was sent as an invalid by rail and boat to England for treatment and convalescence. He was dispatched to St. Georges Hospital south of London where my mother, Joan Foot, a 20-year-old who, having completed her formal education, was there volunteering as a Red Cross Nurse.

The nursing and care and recovery that this 38-year-old wounded soldier received, led to a romance, and eventual marriage in 1916, the birth of my oldest brother Maxwell in 1917. After which they came home to Canada where my mother and dad had nine more children for a total of ten between the period of 1917 to 1931. Now, had it not been for the German Emperor Kaiser, King of Prussia, declaring war on our Allies, causing my father to join the army, go to Valcartier with thousands of men and horses, go to Britain, thence to Europe, then being wounded and the killing of his horse, being sent to St. George's Hospital, and meeting my mother which eventually ended up with **me** being born in 1925 on this old rocky ball called Canada.

A **man's sperm** contains 22 **chromosomes** as well as either an X- or a Y-**chromosome**. A woman's egg contains 22 **chromosomes** plus an X-**chromosome**. The **sperm** that fertilizes the egg determines the baby's sex. If the **sperm** carries an X-**chromosome** the baby will be XX and will become a girl.

Added to the chance which I attempted to outline above of my ending up being a Canadian citizen are the known scientific facts that a birth is brought about when one egg, designated as *Chromosome X,* in the female and 100 million sperm being produced by a male, half of which are *Chromosome X* and the other half are *Chromosome Y,* meet under the right conditions. If the the *X Chromosome* from the male meets up with the *X Chromosome* in the female, then the resulting birth is a female child *XX*, and if a *Y Chromosome* from the male gets home first then you have a male child *XY*.

So, surviving this dilemma and having the luck that one of those 100 million sperm managed to fertilize the egg and the result is YOU is far beyond winning the greatest LOTTO in the world. So considering all these happenings and scientific facts may I humbly state that **'I am here'** to write a book.

Hardships Suffered by Horses in War Time

8,000,000 horses and countless mules and donkeys died in WW1. They were used to transport ammunition and supplies to the front and many died not only from the horrors of shellfire but also in terrible weather and appalling conditions. When the Canadians embarked from Quebec to Britain the horses were in the hold of the ship and one only has to imagine the conditions in that accommodation - the crowding, darkness, movement caused by the rough water, and overall strangeness must have been terrifying for the poor animals.

Considering the hazards and ill treatment of horses one has only to imagine the conditions that these men and horses were exposed to and regardless of man's love of the horse and its welfare, under war conditions the situation was beyond any one person's control. Obviously I had nothing to do with WW1 but I was involved in WW2 and although we did not use horses, the Germans did in a big way. When they occupied France and mainly Belgium, they confiscated their heavy horse population and used them and conscripted Belgian farmers to drive them and they were used to draw equipment such as artillery guns because of their shortage and saving of gasoline. When we became involved in intense fighting in Normandy, in thousands of cases these horses which were under fire and noise, broke loose and almost everywhere we would see loose or wounded or dead horses and, excuse me for being dramatic and factual, but when the Germans and equipment and horses trying to escape were trapped in the Falaise Gap as a result of our encirclement, the two mile gap was strafed my our air command and our Artillery to the point that the road was blocked with more than a thousand dead Germans, equipment and hundred of horses. It took our engineers three days with D8 bulldozers to clear the road which was a sight and had a smell that no young Canadian boy should be witnessing or been subjected to.

Even though the horses would appear to have been neglected, everything possible was done to ensure their welfare in such an unavoidably adverse environment. There was a special unit of graduate veterinarians with qualified horsemen as assistants in a unit called the *Canadian Veterinary Corps* to do everything humanly possible to ensure the welfare of each individual horse under such awful conditions.

Wild Horses

Almost every country has an excess of horses in the wild and in some cases they are a problem and infringe on private lands and more especially on those farmers who have cash crops. How to handle the problem is beyond the ability of any fringe groups who declare themselves as 'Horse Lovers' and go to great lengths to solicit for money from the public to protect their welfare. However, in reality there is absolutely nothing they can do until the governments of the day deal with the problem.

As a veterinarian, on several occasions, at the request of an owner, I have been asked to euthanize or as we say *'Put Down'* a devoted, injured or obsolete horse and I have done this in a very humane manner. I would like everyone who reads this to understand that I, along with every Veterinarian, have an in-depth feeling and respect for the said species.

There is a major problem in areas of the United States where something has to be done but not like yesterday where I read on the computer of a group who are going to do something about preventing slaughter of horses for consumption. In many countries like here in Canada where there are slaughter houses which humanely euthanize horses and freeze the meat for delivery and export to those countries like France who habitually import horse meat for consumption.

You must understand that there are unscrupulous people out there who use this dilemma to pray on so-called *horse lovers* to peel out their money to these, in many cases fraudulent, devious people when in reality their main objective is to put money in their own pockets at the expense of real horse people who are true lovers of the animal.

In one case however the problem is national pride. During a period of time many years ago on Fraser Island, just off the western coast of Queensland, Australia a tremendous supply of lumber was being harvested and horses were extensively used during the harvesting of those trees for consumption on the mainland. When the clearing of the forests was done the horses were left to be free and to this date they run wild there alone with the wild dogs which are called Dingos. No buildings or development of the Island is allowed on what is now a national park and it is great place to visit by ferry to enjoy the wild and beautiful environment. Let me say one more thing regarding wild horses and the problem - when the smoke all settles with Trump and our government, that we sit down and humanely solve the problem using something that many people and nations have forgotten about, that is called 'Common Sense.'

They have a very efficient ferry system crossing from the mainland to Fraser Island and the waters below as they cross is reputed to be the natural breeding areas of the White Whale. This fact has never been proven because anyone who dove down to check that reported fact, never came back. Apparently the captain of the boat tells that humorous anecdote to the travellers each time he crosses.

Equine Contribution to Aviation

One time at a Veterinary convention in Toronto a veterinarian from Norway was giving a talk on his contribution to the development of landing gear on today's aircraft.

When the larger aircrafts, such as those in passenger service were being developed they had a major problem in trial runs with their landing gears. Engineers had several designs built and tested but the problems continued to persist. This veterinarian, who also had a background in the engineering field, came forward with a possible solution after becoming aware of the problems associated in the aviation field.

He advocated a proper functional design, using the same anatomical and landing features of a horse's foot when it comes in contact with the track surface while racing at high speeds. When a horse's foot comes in contact with the racing surface, it lands on its heel, slides forward a couple of inches, then rolls forward onto the foot surface and then it arcs forward and drives on off the toe. At the same time the shock of the landing is transferred up to the ankle, which while the whole weight is placed thereon, is stretched backward and down to almost touching the ground. The remainder of the shock is extended up to the shoulder muscles and joints.

Using this motion as a template the landing gear of an aircraft was adapted so that the two wheels on each side operate in tandem with the rear wheels hanging lower than the front wheels. Thus on landing on the runway the hind wheels take the initial shock and then as the aircraft continues on forward, the front wheels then comes into play to help absorb the weight. Then the shock goes up to a column that copies the ankle of the horse by utilizing mechanical levers using the same anatomical structure of the horse.

All of these foregoing facts is authentic proof that, once again, our equine friend has contributed to our comfort and safety.

A Brief History of Racing in the Ottawa Valley

and Some of the People who have Influenced it and the sport itself

The Ottawa Valley has long had a strong connection to the Standardbred horse and harness racing. It traces back to the long history of ice racing on the Ottawa River behind the parliament buildings and on the slick ice surface of the Rideau Canal following its completion in 1832. Long before Canada was a nation, Ottawa was the ice racing capital of Upper Canada, and attracted the best trotters and pacers from around North America for its annual meetings during the 1800's and early 1900's.

Generations of Valley harness horsemen were born in those early years. They bred, and trained horses on snow-packed country roads in the winter and travelled up and down the Valley, from Pembroke, Shawville, Renfrew, Arnprior and even from the little villages of Cobden and Quyon, Quebec, to race at the one and two-day fair meetings conducted by the agricultural societies.

The races offered very little in purse money for the horse owners, but they were the major attractions at the Valley fall fairs. Each horse raced 3 heats, every heat a race

The season traditionally opened on the 24th of May at Pembroke's O'Kelly Park and it was an exciting time for horsemen to test their green horses and showcase their older campaigners on one of the better maintained Valley tracks.

Names like Alf Switzer, Cecil Champion, Claire Smith, John *Doc* Findley come to mind. They were some of the well known, well respected and successful trainer- drivers in the Valley.

Racing at Quyon was always a day to remember for horsemen travelling there from the Ontario side. The old motorized log raft that was the only form of transportation across the Ottawa River from Fitzroy Harbour to Quyon held only three horses and a few cars and it has been said that sometimes one of the horses would have to swim behind the raft because there was no room on board.

On arrival on the Quebec side the horses became pack animals carrying all of their equipment through the village to the fairgrounds, and with only 10 stalls available, most horses were just tied to a tree and raced from there. Bath water was fetched in pails from the Ottawa River and placed in the sun to warm for the horses' post-race baths.

One of the really nice parts of the day was savouring the delicious meals prepared by the Women's Institute, all for the price of 25 cents.

With the advent of modern day harness racing at the bigger Ontario tracks, harness racing has slowly disappeared from the fall fairs and today in 2018, there is just one fall fair in the province conducting harness racing, and that is at the Six Nations Indian Reservation in Ohsweken, Ontario, near Brantford.

Still, the influence and important contributions of Valley horsemen to the sport has been substantial over the years and continues today.

It is therefore not surprising that one of the largest groups of horsemen from a single geographic area in the Canadian Horse Racing Hall of Fame is from the Ottawa Valley.

T.P. (Tommy) Gorman, J.C. Bert Cameron, Claire Smith, Hector Clouthier, Sr., Dr. John Findley, Bill Galvin and yours truly are all enshrined in the Hall.

Although all were horsemen, they all contributed immensely to the phenomenal growth of the harness racing industry in different ways.

T. P. (Tommy) Gorman

Tommy Gorman was a legendary figure in the North American sporting world and his career spanned a lifetime of extraordinary achievements in horse racing and beyond.

Timer, Racing Secretary, General Manager and then President of Connaught Park, he also found time to act as President of the Province of Quebec Racing Association, guiding racing in that province through the Depression years and the Second World

War at Blue Bonnets, Mount Royal, Dorval, King's Park and Connaught Park. He put life back into Thoroughbred racing at Connaught Park after the First World War, and turned it into a Standardbred operation after making history by racing the first Thoroughbred operation under lights in Canada in 1954.

From racing to hockey, Gorman was never idle. Between racing seasons he won seven Stanley Cups, managing four different teams in five different cities. T.P. (Tommy) Gorman was inducted into the Canadian Horse Racing Hall in the Builders category in 1977.

Tommy Gorman

James, Cuthbert (Bert) Cameron

J.C. (Bert) Cameron, a native of Shawville, Quebec and resident of Smiths Falls, Ont., had a large influence on harness racing and Standardbred breeding in both provinces for a half-century and more starting in the 1930s. He acquired his first harness horse in 1937 in a trade with an old horseman name Bernard Grant. He traded a new truck for some old harness, an old race cart and a horse. According to Cameron, his trainer, Ed McKeller, said the harness and the cart were worth twice as much as the horse.

The Camerons with Ezra Blue

Ezra Blue, Cameron's second purchase in 1938, vaulted him to Canadian harness racing prominence. He paid $250 for Ezra Blue as a three-year-old and campaigned him with distinction for eight years, beginning June 23, 1939 in Chesterville, Ont. It is reported that Cameron said on more than one occasion that his horse helped finance his automobile business during difficult times. Ezra Blue set numerous track records, captured feature races at Saratoga and Roosevelt Raceway, and in 1941 won 21 straight heats while racing at Ontario, Quebec and New York tracks. He was also a successful sire, particularly as a sire of broodmares.

His 500-acre farm near Smiths Falls produced hundreds of top Standardbreds.

One of Ezra Blue's sons, Ezra Deen, was one of Canada's leading pacers during the 1950s. He was the first Canadian-bred horse to earn more than $100,000 for Cameron and raced until he was 14 years of age.

Cameron was the leading breeder of 1976 Ontario Sires Stakes winners and also the leading money-winning owner of Ontario Sires Stakes winners the same year.

In 1974 he was recognized by the Ontario Harness Horsemen's Association as Senior Citizen of the Year for his work and contributions to the Standardbred industry and the sport of harness racing.

James, Cuthbert (Bert) Cameron was inducted into the Canadian Horse Racing Hall of Fame in the Builders category in 1978.

Claire Smith

While a noted horse-man in his own right, it was as an official of the sport that Claire Smith made an indelible mark. He watched the sport grow from a leisurely pastime at Ottawa Valley fairs to a multi-billion dollar industry and he played a significant role in its development.

By the time he was a teenager, the third generation horseman was driving at Ottawa Valley meets. He campaigned throughout the valley in the 1920s, 30s and 40s buying, trading and racing horses as a part-time profession. One of Smith's

Claire Smith

trademarks was his pristine stable. His equipment trunks, harness, horses and horse trailer were always shining and clean. He owned and was involved with many good horses. A full time judge for 24 years, presiding at meets across the country, he left the judges stand in 1985 but continued training horses into his 90s.

During his tenure he served on the Canadian Trotting Association's rules committee and virtually rewrote the rule book.

"Never has there been any judge as fair to the public, the track, and horsemen", said a Toronto newspaper columnist of his work. Smith, who was born in Frankville, Ont, was inducted into the Canadian Horseracing Hall of Fame in the Builders category in 1991. He died in January 2005 at the age of 96.

Dr. John Findley

For a half century and more, a name that resonated harness racing throughout the Ottawa Valley and beyond was "Dr. John (Doc) Findley" and his Arnprior-based Madawaska Farms racing stable and breeding operation.

Since Findley drove his first race at age 13 at the Arnprior fall fair in 1939, he has bred, trained and raced some of the sports outstanding per-formers at both gaits.

Dr. John Findley

The fiercely competitive Findley has enjoyed an auspicious career that spanned five decades and more as a Standardbred breeder, trainer/ driver and veterinarian. Clearly one of the highlights of his professional career came in 1975 when he emerged as the leading percentage driver in North America, a gigantic accomplishment. He also captured 13 different driving titles at various North American tracks during his career.

Due to the size of Findley's Arnprior operation, he hired a number of aspiring young horsemen who, under his tutelage went on to make their mark in the harness sport. Names like Arnprior native Ken Carmichael and Nelson White come to mind.

Dr. John Findley was inducted into the Canadian Horse Racing Hall of Fame in the Trainer/Driver category in 1997. His outstanding, multiple stakes-winning trotting mare, Dalyce Blue, whom he bred, trained and raced, was inducted into the Canadian Horse Racing Hall of Fame in 2012. Dalyce Blue was the first Canadian bred to shatter several long-standing Canadian race records and as a broodmare produced several outstanding trotters.

Hector Clouthier, Sr.,

Born in Petawawa in 1916, Hector Clouthier, Sr., began working for his father's logging company in the Ottawa Valley at age 12 and at 14 was running his own operation. Known as the "Lumber King of the Ottawa Valley" his involvement in the family lumber business continued until his death 75 years later in 2003.

He entered the Standardbred racing industry in 1952, establishing Northwood Stables and the nearby Northwood Hotel in the Pembroke area. He also began a breeding operation that soon expanded to include 40 broodmares and stood three stallions.

Clouthier eventually became involved in racing industry associations, sitting on the boards of the Canadian Trotting Association, the Canadian Standardbred Horse Society and the Ontario Harness

Hector Clouthier, Sr.

Horse Association. It was said that he was one of the founding fathers of organized horsemen in Ontario, helping to negotiate contracts that enabled horsemen to make a career in the racing business. His support and promotion of the industry assisted in the development of Standardbred racing and breeding.

An advocate of stakes races for young horses in Ontario, Clouthier was instrumental in starting discussions for what would become the Ontario Sires Stakes program.

Hector Clouthier, Sr. was inducted into the Canadian Horse Racing Hall of Fame in the Legends category in 2018.

Bill Galvin

Arnprior native William 'Bill' Galvin is a Canadian horse racing historian, poet, author, educator, horseman, humanitarian and a diligent promoter of harness racing, a sport he was introduced to as a 12-year-old by Dr. John Findley at his Arnprior-based Madawaska Farms, co-owned with his father John Findley, Sr.

His promotions transcended horse racing. He was honoured by the Multiple Sclerosis Society of Canada in 1978 when he founded, implemented and was National Coordinator for the Race Against

Bill Galvin

MS, a cooperative fundraising program involving the North American Harness and Thoroughbred industries that raised over $3 million for Multiple Sclerosis research and patient care and provided huge positive mainstream media coverage for the sport across Canada and the US.

Galvin wore many hats in horse racing. He was director of Publicity and Public Relations for the Canadian Trotting Association, a Thoroughbred racing official, director of special promotions (harness and thoroughbred) for the five Ontario Jockey Club tracks, a member of the Advisory Board for the School of Equine Studies at Toronto's

Humber College and conducted equine poetry and art competitions for grade school children.

In 1978 he was named president of the North America Harness Publicists Association and was Course Director for the initial Racing Officials course for Harness racing at Toronto's Humber College of Applied Arts.

He was the founder and coordinator of the provincial and Canadian Intercollegiate Harness Driving Championships, and the World Intercollegiate Harness Driving Championship that attracted college and university students from 10 countries around the world at Toronto's Greenwood Raceway in 1975.

He produced a history of Grand Circuit Racing in Canada, a 100-year history of horse racing at Toronto's Woodbine and Greenwood racetracks, and in 2006 published his best selling *Ballads of the Turf*.

Bill Galvin was inducted into the Canadian Horse Racing Hall of Fame in the Communicator category in 2014. He was presented with his Hall of Fame ring by Dr. John Findley, the man who introduced him to the sport in 1943.

But, Galvin's blockbuster promotion for the sport took place on February 4th 1979 when he founded, coordinated and implemented the historic revival of trotting races on Ottawa's frozen Rideau Canal. It was a unique recreation of a century-old tradition of early Canadian history with modern day harness racing stars. The inaugural event was staged in sub zero temperatures and attracted some of the world's top harness drivers and more than 40,000 spectators, including Prime Minister Pierre Trudeau and his three sons, Justin, Alexandre and Michel. The event attracted 96 journalists and was the feature attraction of Ottawa's now famous Winterlude celebration. The races drew international media attention and live national television and radio coverage and was credited with thrusting that initial edition of Winterlude into prominence among the world's winter carnivals.

Claire Smith was the presiding judge of the ice races on that frigid afternoon.

At that time I was president of the Canadian Trotting Association and worked closely with Bill, who was the Trotting Association's Director of Publicity and Public Relations at the time. The project took an entire year to organize.

Today it is remembered as an iconic day in the long history of the trotting sport in Canada.

But Galvin was not finished promoting the sport following his Hall of Fame induction. In 2015 he founded and implemented *the Stable That God Loves*, a fundraising and public relations initiative for the harness racing industry. Galvin convinced the owners of over 80 trotters and pacers campaigning at some 32 racetracks across the continent gave back to the sport, donating a percentage of their earnings to the homeless Standardbred Racetrack Chaplaincy of Canada that assists the less fortunate in the horseracing workforce in southwestern Ontario. The program attracted major mainstream media attention, drawing national television coverage and was named one of *the 2015 Newsmakers of the Year* by Trot magazine.

In 2017 Galvin and I approached Heritage Canada in an effort to again bring the trotters back to the canal, but were informed that horse racing was not permitted there any more. But in an enthusiastic effort to commemorate that historic event in 1979, Heritage Canada officials implemented a fitting momento that was inserted into their beautiful display of ice carvings during the 2017 Winterlude celebrations in downtown Ottawa's Confederation Park, a national historic site.

Two professional and talented ice carvers from Siberia spent three days carving a life-size commemorative crystalline sculpture of a trotting horse, driver and sulky, from a five-ton block of ice.

The carving, when lit up at night was a magnificent spectacle and was one of the most popular ice carvings in the Park. It was seen and admired by just under a million people, either in person, or on television.

The ice carving.

Again In 2017, the year Canada celebrated its 250th year of horse racing, Galvin was an international ambassador for harness racing when he travelled to Berlin's century-old Mariendorf Raceway for an historic presentation of racing memorabilia to Germany's Horse Racing Hall of Fame, and thereby hangs a tale.

Hans Fromming and his wife, Inge with Roly in 1975

In 1975, German driving ace, Hans Fromming, was invited by Galvin to Toronto's Greenwood Raceway to compete in a driving competition with North America's top harness driver, Herve Filion. It was billed the Battle of the Giants. At the time Fromming was the world's leading dash winner. Following the competition, in an act of friendship and appreciation, Fromming presented Galvin with the silver-tipped whip he had used in the competition. 42 years later, in 2017, Galvin journeyed to Berlin's Mariendorf Racetrack, and in a touching winners circle presentation, returned Hans Fromming's silver- tipped whip to its rightful place in the German Trotting Hall of Fame, where Hans Fromming is an honoured member.

In return, Galvin was presented with two signed whips from German driving ace, and former world's leading dash winner, Heinz Wewering to return to the Canadian Horse Racing Hall of Fame, and one for the U.S. Hall of Fame in Goshen, New York.

The exchange of whips between Canada, Germany and the U.S.A. served as gestures of international cooperation between the three nations, and represented the bond that exists within the sport of harness racing, and the importance of sharing the history of our sport.

The exchange of the whips with John Stapleton, President of the Canadian Horse Racing Hall of Fame, Bill Galvin, Linda Rainey, Managing Director of the Canadian Horse Racing Hall of Fame

I spent many enjoyable moments with Fromming when he visited Toronto for his joust with Herve Filion. At the time I was president of the Canadian Trotting Association.

In 2018 Galvin continued with his promotions for Standardbred breeding and racing with his *Youth Literary Derby*, a juried, horse-themed writing contest designed to encourage writing and literary skills for all students in Ontario grades 5 to 8. The Youth Literary Derby called for students' evaluations and perceptions of the Standardbred horse, challenging the students to express in prose and verse their *up-close* encounters with newborn Standardbred foals they visited at Standardbred breeding farms across the province.

The contest carried $2000 in prize money donated by St. Catharines horseman, Tom Rankin and free tuition for on-line horse courses at the University of Guelph. It drew entries from 46 Ontario villages, towns and cities.

. . . and now about myself:

Dr. Roly Armitage

During 70 plus years as a veterinarian, Standardbred breeder, owner, administrator and race-track manager, I have seen the harness industry emerge from the county fairs where horses raced for a paltry few dollars in the 1930s, 40s and 50s, to today's major racetracks across the country where million dollar purses are up for grabs for the top horses. Standardbreds are going faster these days, much faster, and as a breed they are more handsome, and their training regimen is less strenuous than in the past.

I like to think that I have contributed to the advancement of the Standardbred industry during its steady growth over my 70 years in the sport. I was privileged to sit on the board of the Canadian Trotting Association, harness

Dr. Roly Armitage

racing's governing body, and was president of that national body from 1974 to 1980. During my tenure I was instrumental in introducing electronic eligibility to the sport, putting Canada on the leading edge of technology in horse racing and was also a strong proponent for the freeze branding identification technique of horses that came to be employed by the Standardbred breeding industry.

Since returning from World War 11 where I served with the Royal Canadian Artillery, my roles in the sport and beyond have been many. From 1972 to 1974 I served as president of the Canadian Standardbred Horse Society, was general manager of Rideau Carleton Raceway for nine years, bred and raced Standardbreds. My Armstead Farms Stable campaigned several noteworthy horses over the years and today it is still active and successful under my son Don.

The successful efforts of my year-long battle with racing authorities to remove the hub rail at Canada's racetracks was probably one of the proudest moments and most significant achievements of my life. For years the hub rails caused serious injury and sometimes death to drivers and their horses when accidents occurred during a race and during training sessions.

In 1990 I left Rideau Carleton for the political arena and ran for the Liberal party. I won the nomination but lost by 324 votes in the federal election. I was elected Mayor of West Carleton for a three-year term from 1991 to 1994 and was honoured to be inducted into the Canadian Horse Racing Hall of Fame in the Builders category in 1999 and in 2000 was inducted into the Ottawa Sports Hall of Fame.

Made in the USA
Columbia, SC
06 September 2018